The Joy of Teaching

The Joy of

Peter Filene

Teaching

A practical guide for new College Instructors

FOREWORD BY KEN BAIN

The

University of

North Carolina

Press

Chapel Hill &

London

This book was published with the assistance of the H. Eugene and
Lillian Youngs Lehman Fund of the University of North Carolina Press.
A complete list of books published in the Lehman Series appears at the
end of the book.

This book was published with the assistance of the H. Eugene and
Lillian Youngs Lehman Fund of the University of North Carolina Press.
A complete list of books published in the Lehman Series appears at the
end of the book.

The paper in this book meets the guidelines for permanence and
durability of the Committee on Production Guidelines for Book
Longevity of the Council on Library
Resources.

Library of Congress
Cataloging-in-Publication Data
Filene, Peter G.
The joy of teaching : a practical guide for new college instructors / Peter
Filene ; foreword by Ken Bain.
    p. cm.
Includes bibliographical references and index.
ISBN-13: 978-0-8078-2942-4 (cloth: alk. paper)
ISBN-10: 0-8078-2942-0 (cloth: alk. paper)—
ISBN-13: 978-0-8078-5603-1 (pbk.: alk. paper)
ISBN-10: 0-8078-5603-7 (pbk.: alk. paper)
    1. College teaching—Handbooks, manuals, etc. 2. First year teachers—
Handbooks, manuals, etc. I. Title.
LB2331.F493 2005
378.1′2—dc22   2004019090

cloth   09 08 07 06 05   5 4 3
paper   10 09 08 07   10 9 8 7

To my colleagues

and students,

past and present,

at the University

of North Carolina,

Chapel Hill

Contents

Figures

Foreword   Ken Bain

When I started teaching U.S. political history in college in the 1960s, I knew my subject well, but I knew little about how to help other people learn. Before the first class meeting, the chair of the department gave me a list of the students who had enrolled in the course, told me the room number where the class would meet, and handed me a copy of the departmentally adopted textbook. That's the only help I received. No one gave me any advice on how to set objectives, prepare a syllabus, teach the class, or assess my students' work. My students and I suffered through the semester, constantly struggling to accommodate each other.

Peter Filene has made the journey into college teaching much easier, more productive, and profoundly more enjoyable. He has crafted a succinct guide for new instructors (as he says, "suggestive rather than exhaustive"). To do so, he has drawn from his years of highly successful experience as a history professor at the University of North Carolina, mixed in important ideas from the literature on teaching and learning, and combined it all with the wisdom and practices of his colleagues. One of the distinctive features of this work is the use of illustrations from course materials in a variety of subjects. He offers a nuts-and-bolts book, providing readers with pithy and sage advice on topics as far-ranging as planning a course and surviving the diverse demands of a faculty appointment. He also asks his readers to confront two fundamental questions that may not pop into every professor's mind but the answers to which can, research suggests, make an enormous difference: "What does it mean to be a teacher?" and "How do you view your students and their needs?"

He demonstrates something I've long contended (see, for example, Ken Bain, *What the Best College Teachers Do* [Cambridge, Mass.: Harvard University Press, 2004]): we can learn much from the practices of outstanding college teachers. Filene is a great teacher who has familiarized himself with the vast body of research and theoretical literature on teaching and learning and can, therefore, conceptualize his own practice. Introductions to college teaching have been popping up like mushrooms in recent years, but precious few of them have come from people who have spent several decades successfully fostering their students' learning. Few of those have blended their own insights with the best ideas from both the literature and colleagues.

Filene has a wonderful way with words and a capacity to drive quickly to the heart of the matter. His crisp prose invites readers into a delicious conversation. Usually he doesn't suggest a particular approach. Rather he raises the issue, lays out a variety of examples of what various professors have done—often quoting from syllabi or other course materials—and leaves the reader to make the final choice. He doesn't try to cover everything about teaching and learning but lets readers get started with basic issues and helps them realize that there is much to know about human learning and how best to foster it. Finally, he offers an excellent annotated bibliography, a road map for future study.

New teachers will find in this little volume a systematic introduction to college teaching. More experienced professors will find a host of productive new ideas that will help them improve their efforts. Every reader will find an engaging and friendly discussion and a wealth of stories that both inform and inspire. I've been teaching for many years, explored and contributed to the literature on college teaching, and directed teaching centers at Vanderbilt, Northwestern, and New York Universities, and I found in this book fresh ideas that gave me a renewed sense of the joy of teaching. I highly recommend it to you.

Acknowledgments

Just as teaching involves a dialogue with students, the writing of this book has engaged me in an extended dialogue with colleagues, students, friends, and editors, as well as the writings of scholars. They have enriched this book more than they know.

Let me begin at the beginning. Thomas LeBien showed up in my office one afternoon and gave me the idea for this project. To put it mildly, I am grateful for his gift.

Soon afterward, Ken Bain—director of the New York University Center for Teaching Excellence—volunteered some suggestions, launching an extraordinary two-year-long conversation between us about pedagogy. I value his wisdom as well as his modesty. The book would not be what it is without Ken's contributions.

Ed Neal, at the University of North Carolina Center for Teaching and Learning, gave me astute comments as I struggled to define the project and, throughout, responded generously to my queries.

During my many years of teaching at the University of North Carolina, I have been nurtured and instructed by my fellow teachers—colleagues in the best sense of the word. My fellow historian and friend John Kasson offered his usual incisive, creative comments on an early draft of the manuscript at an early stage. More generally, John has encouraged and guided me as I wrestled with questions large and small, professional and personal.

Michael Salemi, in the Economics Department, provided helpful critiques as well as materials. Sylvia Hoffert's comments greatly improved one chapter. And I'm indebted to Michael Hunt for leading me to my splendid editors at the University of North Carolina Press, Chuck Grench, Amanda McMillan, and Paula Wald.

I am also indebted to several anonymous readers for their patient, scrupulous reactions, as well as to those whom I can thank by name: Harold Berlak for his demanding comments on the initial proposal; and David Voelker, Robert Johnston, and Lee Warren for cogent critiques of the manuscript. Although I have resisted some of their suggestions, they have made the book immensely better.

Halfway through the project, I had the good fortune of a semester's fellowship at the University of North Carolina Institute for the Arts and Humanities. In our Tuesday afternoon colloquia, faculty from various departments animatedly exchanged constructive ideas. They broadened my intellectual horizons and made the book interdisciplinary. I want to thank Sahar Amer, Daniel Anderson, Bill Barney, Lucia Binotti, Philip Gura, Laura Janda, Susan Klebanow, Tim Marr, Peter Redfield, Rashmi Varma, Jessica Wolfe, Julia Wood, and the Institute's director, Ruel Tyson.

On every page of this book I have drawn upon innumerable conversations with my colleagues and students at the University of North Carolina, as well as the people at the Center for Teaching and Learning. In particular, I have learned immeasurably from the many faculty and graduate students with whom I have worked since 1980 in the History Department's Committee on Teaching.

Years ago, Gerhard Weinberg induced me to overcome my inhibitions and to teach graduate students. I'm so glad he did. Since then, I've regularly taught a graduate seminar on "Designing an Undergraduate Course," the seedbed of this book. While writing the final chapters, I happened to be teaching the seminar again. The students served as an early audience and provided thoughtful evaluations. My thanks to Michael Allsep, Glen Feighery, David Holdzkom, Michael Kramer, Pamella Lach, Paul Quigley, Robert Richardson, Nancy Schoonmaker, Sarah Shurts, and Montgomery Wolf.

Finally, and always, I thank Erica Rothman. As part of our endlessly interesting marriage, this book has been nourished by her wonderful intelligence, sensibility, and penchant for asking questions.

The Joy of Teaching

Introduction

Welcome to your first year of teaching. This book will serve, I hope, as a travel guide to accompany you through the opportunities and quandaries that you'll experience as you launch your career. We will spend most of the time on the challenges that will occupy most of *your* time: developing and teaching your courses. But we'll also consider extracurricular matters that deal with how you relate to your students and colleagues.

I won't dictate "the right answers." Not only do teachers vary in their goals, styles, and values, but they also work in diverse contexts, ranging from three-hundred-person courses to ten-person seminars and from research universities to community colleges. So this book will describe a variety of approaches to expand your options.

Along the way I will cite empirical studies to help you weigh the advantages and disadvantages of various pedagogical strategies. While the research on human learning and teaching does not offer definitive "answers," it does provide useful perspectives. There's no need to reinvent the wheel. Rest assured, though. You are not expected to become a cognitive psychologist. Rather, I address you as a reflective professional, someone who is able to think deeply about your teaching and talk about it conceptually with colleagues.

This is a short guidebook—suggestive rather than exhaustive. If you want to read more, consult the annotated bibliography. But I assume you have precious little time, even to read a book designed to help you improve your teaching and avoid wasting time. So each chapter will be not only succinct and practical, but encouraging as well as enjoyable.

I also want to relieve you of the burden of "getting it right" the first time. Even experienced professors need three run-throughs to fashion a course to their satisfaction. The first time is trial and error, when you discover what's possible and what's not.

(Think back to the first drafts of your graduate school seminar papers.) The second time you teach the course, you avoid the initial errors and false turns (like writing the second draft of that seminar paper). Then—and only then—you can take the content for granted and step back to ponder the structure and process. So the third rendition of the course is what you dreamed of: coherent, well-paced, incisive. And even then, ideally you will never stop finding new angles and additions.

Does this mean you should resign yourself to two rounds of ineptitude? On the contrary. While the journey may be bumpy and erratic at times, you will have a special bond with your students because you, like them, will be taking the course for the first time. Together you'll contend with the excitement and unpredictability (and yes, anxiety) of learning.

This brings me to a fundamental pedagogical principle of the guidebook. When you teach, you are *engaging in a relationship* with your students. That's perhaps too obvious to mention. On the other hand, as you sit down to plan your course, you may become so enthralled with organizing the content that you forget about the 30 or 130 people who will be looking at you that first day. After spending so many years of apprenticeship, you are probably impatient to stand at the lectern. You envision provocative lectures and probing discussions of the monographs that inspired you. But the vast majority of undergraduates are not taking your course to become historians, psychologists, philosophers, or whatever you are. Some enjoy history as presented by the History Channel. Some expect Psych 101 to help them achieve self-fulfillment; others are required to take the course.

In this guidebook I will persistently remind you that teaching is a two-way process, what education scholars call "dialogic." An instructor talks, but what do his or her students hear and understand? Teaching is only as successful as the learning it produces. Indeed, the teaching/learning relationship is not simply dialogic, between professor and student, but polylogic, among students, too. They may learn from each other, or intimidate each other, but positively or negatively, tacitly or explicitly, they play their role in the pedagogical relationship. Together, students and professor interact with the other member of this process: namely, the subject matter.[1]

Please don't misread me. In emphasizing this interactive process, I am not implying that students' expectations and practices should determine your own. The purpose of teaching is not to satisfy consumers' wishes or to find the lowest common denominator. Because learning involves venturing beyond what one already knows and believes, an effective teacher takes students out of their "comfort zone." He or she challenges them with unsettling ideas, sets high standards, demands introspection and hard work—all the while, heeding how students are responding.

In this three-way relationship among themselves and with their subject matter, teacher and students aspire to create what one may call *a learning environment*. They collaborate on a quest in which they are propelled by curiosity, study evidence, react and discuss and interrogate, and finally arrive at various understandings. I recall, for example, one afternoon when the students in my freshman seminar were discussing André Malraux's novel, *Man's Fate*. After two intense hours I suggested a break. "Not yet," they protested. "First we have to figure out: what *is* man's fate?"

How does a teacher produce this kind of environment? You raise questions that you want to pursue, questions that you find intriguing, important, and beautiful. But as the following chapters will help you to accomplish, you need to frame those questions in ways that appeal not just to scholars, but to students who are newcomers to your field.

A metaphor will dramatize those abstractions and also define my principles. Teaching should not be like pitching a baseball toward a student in the batter's box to see whether he/she hits or strikes out. Ideally, a teacher organizes a game of Frisbee, inviting students to catch an idea and pass it on.[2]

For me, teaching at its best is a joyful kind of work. I want to help you have a similar experience.

part One

Premises

1 / Understanding Yourself as a Teacher

When most novice (and not-so-novice) instructors start to plan a course, they focus with varying degrees of excitement and anxiety on the subject matter. But in doing so they are leapfrogging two crucial questions: "Why do you want to teach?" and "What kind of a teacher do you want to be?" These may seem to be an unduly personal detour en route to your syllabus. As thousands of studies have suggested, however, good teachers display five characteristics that depend less on scholarly expertise than on personal skills.

Enthusiasm ranks first on the list. Good teachers care about their subject with zest and passion, and they enjoy communicating it to others.

To communicate effectively, good teachers present their ideas with *clarity*. Rather than the nuances and sophistication used when conversing with peers, they highlight the central themes in language that nonprofessionals can understand.

To accomplish clarity requires *organization*.

With sufficient clarity and organization—and also enthusiasm—good teachers lay the groundwork for *stimulating* their students, arousing their desire to learn.

Finally, good teachers *care* about their students. They treat students fairly, want them to succeed, give them respect, and offer support.[1]

Let me quickly state that I am not prescribing how you should teach. Professors will enact these criteria in all sorts of ways. The activity of teaching embodies one's deeply individualized, even idiosyncratic traits and values. My purpose is to help you realize yours. This chapter seeks to inspire—or at least nudge—you to reflect upon the style, mode of inquiry, and values that you bring to your classroom. With that in mind, consider the following assortment of pedagogical personas.

Fall is Mr. Rothschild's favorite season because each fall he gets to start anew [teaching history at Scarsdale High School, Scarsdale, New York]. Last fall, engaging students in a discussion of the American Revolution, the trim, gray-haired, 54-year-old dashed around the classroom like the high school soccer fullback he once was, waving his arms excitedly at students' ideas and questions, especially their questions.
Wrong answers are fine—no, better than fine. "That's a *great* wrong answer!" he'll exclaim.
Exclamations are his hallmark.[2]

You may have enjoyed dramatic professors like Rothschild: perhaps the one who sang spirituals to your folklore class, or the one who dressed in armor while lecturing on the Crusades. But if you're shy, or if your brand of humor tends toward understated wit, those models will only get in your way.

At the other end of the stylistic spectrum, you may have been awed by an erudite scholar who lectured eloquently for an hour about Hegelian theories of progress, without a glance at either his students or his notes.

There was something about [Berkeley history professor Frederick J.] Teggart's appearance and his manner of entering the lecture room and striding to the rostrum that silenced student conversation instantly. Never once did he have to wait a moment or two, as most of us do, for the chatter to cease and newspapers be put down. Not that he was in any way overbearing. He was simply the essence of academic man in his bearing, with a natural dignity that no one was likely to wish to encroach upon. . . . He lectured from brief, penciled notes on a single sheet of paper. I learned later, when I was his graduate assistant in the course, that he prepared these during the hour or two before his lecture. . . . He had remarkable powers of recall while on his feet, and he seemed to have no difficulty whatever in building his spare, telegraphic notes into sentences and paragraphs which, from both style and content, might have been prepared word for word in advance. I once asked him why, in order to save energy, he hadn't spent some early year typing his lectures for reuse. All he said was, "Never type your lectures; you and the students will both be their slaves."[3]

But you may be the kind of teacher who is nourished by the back-and-forth of discussion. In any case, why add to the anxiety of a new course by pretending that you can navigate a complex hour-long presentation by memory? Surely Lewis and Clark would have taken a map with them if there were a map to be had.

In contrast to Professor Teggart, then, contemplate Socrates. In the movie *The Paper Chase*, John Houseman (as a Harvard Law School professor) enacts a merciless Socratic pedagogy. In real-life classrooms, such teachers often make lifelong impressions upon their students.

I began my teaching career, as many of us do, hoping to imitate my favorite and most exciting college teacher. The master whom I hoped to emulate was an expert in conducting the Socratic dialogue. His classes were experiences in insight, and in terror. We came to class braced and ready to try to answer his questions intelligently, always fearful that we might give a stupid answer. . . . No one dared attend without having read the texts assigned. He would begin with the simplest of questions: in a class on the "Rime of the Ancient Mariner," for example, he insisted that the important question was the simplest one, "Why did the Mariner kill the bird?" And from leading us to consider that obvious first step, he proceeded to show us Coleridge's depiction of the mysteries of choice, of fault, and of salvation. One of the epiphanal moments of my intellectual life came at the end of that class when, having followed his line of argument throughout, I was left with the ineluctable answer: "He killed the bird because he *wanted* to."[4]

To be sure, the Socratic method isn't necessarily intimidating. Socrates himself is gentle and patient in the *Dialogues*. Nor does the method have to direct students step by step. What do you think about this approach by a renowned teacher in the field of music?

Someone—I think the cellist Bernard Greenhouse—has left a picture of Pablo Casals teaching. Knees to knees with the young cellist, Casals plays a phrase from the Bach unaccompanied suites, and then pauses while the student plays it. "No," Casals says, and plays it again. The student plays it again. "No," Casals says, this time perhaps with a comment or a joke, and plays it again. And so on for the whole lesson.[5]

Your style and your mode of inquiry have implications for human values. There are different kinds of values, of course—intellectual, political, moral—but to some extent they all come into play in the classroom. One teacher may model dispassionate "objectivity." Another may want students to appreciate the beauty and power of the subject matter. A third may try to shake up students' complacency, challenging their conventional wisdom and, in turn, urging them to challenge his or hers. A fourth may hope to make students "feminist" or "conservative." Which one of these goals, or which combination, do you find most in keeping with your values?[6]

Likewise, think about how you want students to deal with one another. If you set ground rules that reward supportive and cooperative interactions, you foster one type of classroom culture. Ground rules that reward competitive and individualistic behavior encourage a different type of culture.

Some excellent teachers lecture, some interrogate, and others coach. Some are fierce, others gentle. Some teach history (or economics or literature, etc.); some teach students; and most do both in varying proportions. Everyone incorporates certain values.

Which type of teacher are you? As a means of explicating your style, mode of inquiry, and values, complete the following five prompts.[7] If metaphors or scenarios spring to mind, use them as a means toward (or instead of) abstract answers.

- I bring to teaching a belief that _____.
- In the classroom I see myself as _____.
- I believe students are _____.
- I seek to foster in students _____.
- I think learning is _____.

Needless to say—but I'll say it anyhow—your answers are preliminary. As you test them upon actual students in actual classrooms day after day, semester after semester, you'll know a lot more about how and why you choose to teach. You will refine or even discard the model you set out with, just as Jackson Pollock eventually stopped imitating his mentors and painted like Pollock. Such was the case for Mary Burgan, whom I quoted earlier as a would-be Socratic teacher. "Slowly . . . I reached some painful conclusions," she realized. "I was not temperamentally cut out to be a Socratic questioner." Her mentor could happily lead students toward the right answer (like Casals's "no, no"), but "I was a coward. I could never bring myself to tell a student that he or she was *wrong*."[8]

You may be wondering, then: Why go to the trouble of defining a philosophy prematurely, before acquiring real-life evidence? But the question rests on a false assumption. Not even the greenest beginner proceeds via pure induction. Whether consciously or unconsciously, each of us works with some notions of what we think is good (and bad) pedagogy.[9] So the more that you can put those notions out in front of yourself, the more likely you will design a course that fits *you* rather than a teacher you admire.

This process of self-reflection will also benefit your students. As participants in the teaching/learning relationship, they will busily interpret every clue as to who you are, how you work, and what you expect of them. The more clearly you spell out that information—defining yourself as a teacher—the more effectively they can work with you.

Here is how a seasoned professor has defined his teaching philosophy—in effect, his answers to the five prompts I listed earlier. I hope it gives you a sounding board for thinking about your own pedagogy.

In teaching, I seek to impart a desire among students to learn more about the subject I am offering; to press them to question established canons, their own beliefs, and popular representations of Russia; and to design strategies that help students appreciate the power and benefits of thinking *historically*. I strive to reach my goals by creating a classroom environment that is nurturing and invites students to take risks but at times may make them a bit uncomfortable by expecting them to be prepared. In embracing a holistic approach to learning, I also want my students to take away from courses skills that will help them in other classes and in life—reading critically, writing lucidly, and identifying an author's argument, use of evidence, biases, and/or silences. I push them to value different kinds of historical evidence and texts; to articulate reasoned arguments of their own; and to use the Internet. . . . I premise my pedagogical strategies on the assumption that students need to feel that they can succeed in my courses and understand what they will be responsible for. I strive to be passionate and well-organized about my teaching.[10]

In conclusion, I want to make two quick and crucial points. First, no teacher closes this chapter once and for all. Personal identity is a *process*, not a formula. As one inhabits new stages of life and new roles, one's sense of self evolves. However you define yourself as a teacher now, you will redefine it in the course of years and courses to come.

Second, just as teaching is relational, so is identity. You have to be true to yourself, but you also have to take into account who your students are. That subject deserves a chapter of its own.

2 / Understanding Your Students

Teaching is an interactive process, whether it involves Pablo Casals and a student sitting knees to knees or a professor orating to 350 people. The size of a class matters. But that is only the most visible circumstance shaping the pedagogical relationship. A teacher also needs to take into account less visible and even invisible circumstances. In this chapter we will discuss six factors ranging from academic to economic.

Consider first the academic expectations that your students bring to the classroom. What kind of *campus culture* are you dealing with? Is this an intellectual environment? a "party school"? a commuter school where students come from their day jobs to become credentialized one course at a time? Are students strongly politicized? religious? conservative? Here the newcomer to campus is at a disadvantage. But you can acquire at least a general impression by asking your colleagues what to expect. (At the same time, beware of turning an impression into a stereotype, which then becomes a self-fulfilling prophecy.)

- How many pages of reading per week does one typically assign?
- What is the typical distribution of grades?
- Is absenteeism a problem?
- Do students begin their weekend on Thursday night or Friday?
- Do most students live in dorms or off-campus?
- How many are employed in full- or part-time jobs that limit their opportunity to do academic work?[1]
- How many have children or other pressing family obligations?

- How do they react to political or other controversial topics being raised in class?

Then there are questions of *academic preparation*. What have your students already learned about ancient China, Shakespeare, or the Supreme Court? Here you can find answers easily enough by handing out a diagnostic quiz (unsigned, ungraded) on the first or second day of class. The trouble is, of course, that you have to order books, write some lectures, and plan discussions now, before knowing the results of that diagnostic. You should therefore build in contingency plans. For example, define a few classes as "TBA" (to be announced) in case you need to proceed more slowly than expected. Anticipate which assignments to whittle down if your students find the work load too difficult.

In addition, there are the amorphous but crucial questions not about what your students know, but about what they *think* they know. Students' minds are not blank slates. Having seen *Forrest Gump*, they're sure that all hippies were in league with violent antiwar protesters. Even if they rate Picasso as "great," they may dismiss abstract art as "something my six-year-old sister could paint."

Mental models such as these shape how students will understand what we tell them. You may declare again and again that "the past is a foreign country; people do things differently there." But students—like all humans—use their existing models of reality to understand anything new. Students will try to understand Japanese family life, for example, in terms of what they think they know about how their own world works. Before they can learn what you want to teach, they need to become aware of and then unlearn what is already scribbled on their minds. If you want them to abandon their current mental model and build a new one (or at least recognize the problem of entertaining two competing paradigms) you need to create two conditions. First, you need to put the students in a situation where their existing model doesn't work (what the learning literature calls an "expectation failure"). Second, students then have to care that their model doesn't work, and care enough to stop and grapple with their quandary.

In other words, you need to listen before you begin professing.

Figure 2.1. One-Minute Feedback Memo

The main point of today's class is

What interested me most is

What I don't understand is

    Name (optional) _____

Otherwise, you'll be frustrated by students' resistance or confusion and mistakenly blame them or, worse, blame yourself. I recommend several remarkably easy ways to discover students' preconceptions:

- Begin class by asking, "What comes to your mind when I say 'Africa' [or 'hippies,' 'Freud,' etc.]?" Or, as you begin a lecture on colonial New England, ask students to describe a typical Puritan. Or employ my favorite, surefire, discussion opener, which is both nonthreatening and revealing: "What in today's reading surprised you?"
- Call for a vote in order to gauge the mental temperature of the class: "Here's a painting by Grandma Moses and one by Willem de Kooning. Which do you prefer, and why?" or "Dropping the atomic bomb on Hiroshima: yes or no?"
- At the end of class, or halfway through, ask them to fill out a one-minute feedback memo—an $8\frac{1}{2}'' \times 4''$ handout that you can reproduce by the hundreds (see Figure 2.1).

Students' learning is affected not only by their expectations and preparation, but by what one may loosely call their "learning style." Most undergraduates prefer to learn in groups rather than on their own. As a result, they are more comfortable and effective in discussions than in lectures. Moreover, they tend to grasp concrete facts more readily than abstract concepts or theories. So they learn more easily when given specific, structured assignments: for example, "define . . ." or "state three reasons for . . ." rather than "explain the significance of . . ." or "apply Piaget's theory to. . . ."[2] These undergraduates' inclinations or preferences run contrary to how their teachers typically prefer to learn. If you're a typical scholar in the humanities and social sciences, you not only are used to sitting alone doing research and writing; you are also practiced in deploying abstractions and theory. That is how and why you have become a scholar. To communicate effectively with most of your students, however, you need to give them opportunities to learn collaboratively (see chapters 6 and 7), and you will do well to anchor lofty concepts in concrete examples (see chapter 5).

In addition to campus culture, academic preparation, mental models, and learning styles, you need to be aware of your students' *stage of cognitive development*. After years of liberal arts training, you understand that the interesting questions have many plausible answers and that "truth" is a contested, if not illusory goal. Your students, on the other hand, and especially your first-year students, will not understand that. In fact, many will find that position unbearably unsettling or just plain wrong, and they will feel confused, resentful, perhaps hostile. The "dialogue" then becomes two sets of minds passing each other in the dark.

Here is how William G. Perry, author of a classic study, *Forms of Intellectual and Ethical Development in the College Years* (1970), portrays the quandary:

Let's start with one of the ordinary enigmas—students' persistent misreading of examination questions. Perhaps "unreading" would be a better term. We commonly struggle in staff meetings for nearly an hour over the wording of an essay question for the mid-term. . . . At last the issue is stated clearly, concisely, and unambiguously. Yet, if the class contains a large contingent of freshmen, the blue books will reveal that a third of the students looked at the question to locate the topic and ignored all the rest of the words, so carefully crafted. It will seem as if these students read the question as saying: "Tell all you know about . . ." and then did so, sometimes with remarkable feats of irrelevant memory.[3]

According to Perry, a typical undergraduate passes through a series of cognitive stages. Here is a simplified, four-step summary:

1. *Dualism*—The student sees the world in polar terms of Right and Wrong. So he/she believes learning requires simply taking notes, memorizing the professor's or authors' statements, and recapitulating ("regurgitating") them on the exam. If the professor says there are several possible answers or asks for the student's own interpretation, the student believes the teacher is (perversely) withholding the "right" answer.

2. *Relativism*—After repeated experience dealing with multiple interpretations, the student's dualism erodes and he/she replaces a belief in Truth with a cynical perspective. If there is more than one answer, then knowledge becomes "just my opinion," and everyone's interpretation is as valid as anyone else's, including the teacher's.

3. *Multiplicity*—After teachers have repeatedly called for evidence and reasons to support interpretations, the student recognizes that some positions are truer than others. Now he/she acknowledges complexity, can tolerate ambiguity, and begins to set ideas into context. Or, to put that in somewhat cynical terms, he/she has learned to play the academic game: "I can give the teacher what he/she wants."

4. *Commitment*—Finally, the student internalizes these understandings and transplants them from the classroom to the world at large. He/she has recognized the need to make choices and to commit oneself to those choices. In so doing, he/she integrates the rational, disinterested academic process with her or his experiential, affective life.[4]

More recently, the authors of *Women's Ways of Knowing* have modified Perry's categories according to *gender*. They note that some students in the later stages are "Connected Knowers" while others are "Separate Knowers." The Separate Knowers (who tend to be men) are the adversarial students so prized by most academics. They like to detach themselves from an idea, remaining objective or even skeptical, and are always willing to argue. In contrast, Connected Knowers (who tend to be women) look at the merits of other people's ideas instead of trying to shoot them down. Rather than striving to be dispassionate, unbiased observers, they deliberately bias themselves in favor of the thing they are examining. They believe truth to be embedded in context—approximate instead of absolute—so they pose questions rather than assertions.[5]

One should be wary, however, of seeing students through these binocular lenses. As a communications studies scholar (and feminist) has noted, we simplify the complexity of classroom interactions if we flatten them into male/female dichotomies.[6] Indeed, a narrowly gendered view of students all too easily creates a self-fulfilling prophecy. We may reinforce female students who "connect" while ignoring or discouraging those who offer critical arguments, and vice versa for male students. Gender is only one of many variables at work.[7]

Economic class makes a significant difference. If you are about to teach at a community college or at a university that accepts 90 percent of applicants, your students will likely come from working-class backgrounds. They may be going to school while working in low- to middle-wage jobs and perhaps raising children. As a result, they contend with obstacles that most twenty-year-old middle-class students don't face. According to a sociologist at the University of South Dakota, for example, where two out of five students are nontraditional and the average age is thirty-five or older: "These students have got family problems up to their ears, work obligations, schedules that would boggle anybody's mind. As a consequence, they have legitimate reasons for missing appointments, not coming to class. You know, their kids get sick. There is a crisis in the family. Divorces are going on. . . . I have a very difficult time keeping classes coherent because of the ongoing disruptions."[8]

On the positive side, nontraditional students bring experiences that enrich a classroom in remarkable ways. An instructor of a night class at the Cocoa campus of the University of Central Florida reports:

I have seldom had a more interesting in-class discussion than the one in which a 25-year-old who earns cash spinning electronic

dance music at local clubs squared off against a 60-year-old former NASA employee on the subject of Lyndon Johnson's War on
Poverty. The "youngster," a staunch Republican, was holding forth
on the benefits brought by the free market. His fellow student
jumped in with, "Look, I grew up in Appalachia and my family
was too poor to send me to college, and I wasn't able to afford it
until now, and you kids just don't understand. . . ." Needless to
say, it's not the same kind of conversation that you get with 19-
year-olds.[9]

Working-class students may also have a classroom style that
differs from what you're used to. For example, *discourse.* Most academics reward students who use precise terminology and fluid
sentences replete with subclauses (such as the one you're reading), while deprecating those who speak about "stuff" that is
"really cool" in the book.

Furthermore, as bell hooks has observed, "students from
upper- and middle-class backgrounds are disturbed if heated exchange takes place in the classroom. Many of them equate loud
talk or interruptions with rude and threatening behavior. Yet
those of us from working-class backgrounds may feel that discussion is deeper and richer if it arouses intense responses."[10]

According to a professor of English composition at a community college in New York City, his working-class students are
"largely unimpressed by professors and intellectuals, not easily
persuaded, not pushovers (my doctorate, rank, authority, politics,
and publications don't awe most of them)."[11]

When students' identity as an *ethnic or racial minority* overlaps
their class background, classroom dynamics become even more
complex. Cultural minorities may be self-conscious, more easily
intimidated by their professor or their classmates, and less ac-
customed to open-ended questions. Whereas middle-class whites
can easily take their race and attendant privilege for granted, minority students cannot. They will react differently, sometimes defensively or angrily. An African American professor recalled this
incident from his course in general psychology:

Some years ago, early in the semester . . . , two black women complained to me that they were upset by several things happening in class. They felt most aggrieved by white students repeatedly addressing each of them by the other one's name. I suggested that bringing their feelings up in the class might occasion a learning experience for everyone—"just what we are there for." They did, and they explained to their classmates that such mistakes disturbed them because they harked back to the notion that whites think "all black people look alike" . . . . I did not expect the defensiveness from white students that followed: "You are being too sensitive," "That's a natural mistake," and "I've never been good at names." More disturbing to me were the comments directed to one of the black students: "I consider you distant, arrogant, and condescending," and "You addressed me by the wrong name once, too." Finally, most disturbing were the comments, "I have many friends [relatives, etc.] who are black [people of color]," "I resent being thought of as a racist," and "Some things you have said in class suggest to me that you are homophobic." . . . The discussion deteriorated into an exchange of accusations.[12]

Class, ethnicity, and race make a difference in the pedagogical dialogue. But what that difference is and means is highly variable and subjective. So we need to beware of stereotyping an individual student in terms of his or her group identity. As one African American student tartly remarked to his teacher: "Jesse Jackson doesn't speak for me, Louis Farrakhan doesn't speak for me, Toni Morrison doesn't speak for me. *I* speak for me."[13]

I worry that by now you are feeling paralyzed. How in the world is one supposed to teach subject matter while navigating among dualists, Connected Knowers, ethnic minorities et al.? Here are three recommendations.

(1) *Beforehand*, design your course in order to address these cognitive and experiential differences. For example, you might plan diverse types of assignments:

- some that call for right answers ("Locate on the map . . ." or "Calculate the standard deviation of . . ."), and others that are open-ended ("If you were Lyndon Johnson's Secretary of Defense in 1964, what would you advise him to do in Vietnam?");

- some that are visual ("Design a memorial for the Persian Gulf War") or aural ("Interview a town council candidate"). (For a more detailed discussion, see chapter 7.)

To address differences of gender, ethnicity, and class, incorporate texts and examples that represent a wide range of perspectives. You might pair a conservative article with a liberal one, or invite a colleague whose views disagree with yours to teach one class. You might supplement a monograph with a memoir, novel, or documentary film that recreates experience beyond what you find familiar.[14]

(2) *During the course*, you can employ a variety of early-warning devices that signal what is going on inside students' heads. Instead of waiting until the exam to find out whether they've "gotten" the lectures and readings, solicit feedback along the way. You might distribute the one-minute feedback memo or a wider-ranging evaluation form. Or, devise a more pointed diagnostic, in effect an (ungraded) short-answer quiz: "In no more than twenty-five words, summarize the basic disagreement between Darwinists and creationists." (For further discussion, see chapter 8.)

(3) Despite your best efforts, you may run into trouble. By "trouble" I mean, for example:

- Your dutiful front-row students complain that they're bewildered by your lectures.
- Half the class earned "D's" on the first essay exam.
- The absentee rate is rising.
- Only a handful speak up in discussions.
- Three students send you unsigned notes complaining about your "bad language."

Rather than blaming the students or blaming yourself, diagnose the situation in the light of the various factors I've mentioned:

- Are the students who have difficulty predominantly first-years? If so, what degree of intellectual ambiguity are you setting?

- Are they predominantly of a particular ethnic, economic, or social group? If so, have you collided with their mental model?
- Are they predominantly female? If so, do you reward argumentative comments more than tentative or compassionate ones?
- Have you anchored your concepts in concrete examples?
- Have you accompanied each lecture with a methodical outline?

Teaching is more complicated than a relationship with your accountant and less complicated than marriage, but complicated it is. That's why it's not simply a craft but an art. It's also why, after more than seventy-five semesters in college classrooms, I still find the process deeply and creatively interesting.

In your first semester, chances are you'll run into quandaries, make some mistakes, and spend some sleepless nights brooding about them. But if you muster enthusiasm, preparation, and self-reflectiveness, I'm confident that you'll enjoy the honeymoon.

3 / Defining Your Aims and Outcomes

Now that you have reflected upon yourself and your students, it's time to begin constructing the course. Your initial task is to define the two halves of the teaching/learning dialogue: *aims* and *outcomes*. On the one hand, you want to convey crucial aspects of your subject in lucid, interesting fashion. On the other hand, you want to change how your students think and feel because that is the sine qua non of learning. But what exactly do you mean by these two purposes, and how exactly will you accomplish them?

In my experience, professors have difficulty focusing on outcomes. They prefer to talk about what they themselves will do instead of what their students will do. This chapter will help you keep in mind both sides of the process: teaching and learning. This double-awareness is elusive but also crucial. For if you know what learning looks like, you have a better chance of determining how to foster it.

As a way to grasp this slippery perspective, imagine that you're drafting a "promising syllabus."[1] Think of it as a set of *promises* you're making to your students, promises about

- what they will understand and do (aims and outcomes);
- how you and they will go about achieving these goals (lectures, discussions, writing assignments, etc.);
- how you and they will understand your collaborative progress in learning (evaluation and grading).

This is not just a semantic sleight of hand. By recasting the framework, you'll find it easier to design a course that combines teaching with learning.

We will discuss the second and third "promises" in later chapters. In this chapter let me work with you in explicating the aims and outcomes—that is, in answering two questions:

1. Which ideas or themes do you want to teach? Or to rephrase that in dialogic terms: What kinds of questions will your students be better prepared to answer as a result of taking your course?
2. What kinds of skills will your course help them develop in order to answer those questions?

This exercise will be tentative, of course, and will likely veer toward the vague or the grandiose. Moreover, after spelling out your aims and outcomes, you may decide to keep some of them to yourself. You may wish to state explicitly, for example, your desire that students learn to love nineteenth-century French novels, but not to declare the hope of making students less passive consumers of television. In any case, the process of drafting your pedagogical purposes will give you a mental map as you proceed to the specific components of your course.

To prime the pump of your thinking, consider how professors variously describe their aims and outcomes in their syllabi.

INTRODUCTION TO LABOR ECONOMICS

This course is a study of economic and institutional factors affecting labor demand and supply, the determinants of wages, income and working conditions, and issues of employee compensation and productivity. An overview of the U.S. labor market; neoclassical theory of human capital; the marginal productivity theory of income distribution; an analysis of substitution and income effects on household decision to work; the effects of income taxation on labor supply; an analysis of minimum wage laws [and] theories of discrimination; unions and collective bargaining; and worker mobility and immigration are also covered. Students are required to demonstrate an advanced oral and written proficiency in the literature and research in labor economics.[2]

This bare-bones preface typifies what many professors provide. As one of my colleagues—a devoted and enormously effective teacher—exclaimed, "Why waste my energy and the department's supply budget by spelling out my pedagogical premises and goals in a lengthy document? Students won't read it, and even if they did, they won't make sense of it. What they want to know is how many exams and reading assignments they'll have and how they'll be graded."

True enough. A syllabus is a contract between teacher and student, so you need to define nitty-gritty matters such as assignments, grades, and attendance policy. But pedagogical philosophy serves an equally important purpose, if not for your novice students, then for novice you. After traveling twenty-some times through her course, my colleague knows the route. She has rehearsed and refined her goals. Before you jump in for the first time, on the other hand, you'll do better if you define where you're heading and why. Once you're underway, writing tomorrow morning's lecture while grading last week's exams and worrying about a student who has had a car accident, you'll have no time for such luxurious reflection.

Read, then, an example that is a radical contrast to the preceding one. In this syllabus, the professor begins with a single-spaced page-long explication of the theoretical underpinnings in her course. Here's an excerpt:

POSTCOLONIAL LITERATURES FROM AFRICA,

THE CARIBBEAN, AND SOUTH ASIA

The continuing homogenization of culture, propelled by economic and technological globalization, makes English now perform the task of consolidating cross-national class as well as political alliances. But against the pervasive triumphalism of the planetary reach of "Global English," the course will take the view that in fact the English novel is mapped in very specific historical and material ways, is "broken" into myriad forms whose teaching and reception are always at odds with, while implicated in, the prevailing global order. These fissures of textual effects, writing practices, aesthetic agendas, and pedagogical politics articulate the relations and tensions within and between contemporary English novels.

The English text in this course will be opened up to interrogation to reveal its material and ideological moorings in complex historical processes.[3]

Somewhere between terseness and elaborateness you will make the choice that suits you. Remember, you can't accomplish everything—not in a course lasting fifteen weeks or less, and not on your first journey through. So I recommend this rule of thumb. After devising a wish list, pick the *two* goals and *two* outcomes that matter most to you. For example, you might promise that students will (1) understand "cultural lag" and the symbolic meaning of wars, and (2) learn to read texts critically and also to write thesis statements. Of course you will deal with many other matters along the way. But by spotlighting your purposes and returning to them constantly, you will help your students and yourself. Learning grows by repetition.

The following excerpt from a syllabus may be helpful. In two paragraphs the professor highlights the *key themes* and goes on to describe the *processes* by which students will learn them. If you were an undergraduate in his classroom on the first day, does this preview tell as much as you need to know about his basic objectives?

INTRODUCTION TO POLITICAL PSYCHOLOGY

This course offers a broad introduction to the new, interdisciplinary field of political psychology. It explores the interaction between psychological and political processes. How do citizens think, feel, and behave in the political realm? The course will focus on psychology and political theories, applying them to political behavior at both the elite and mass levels.

The course also seeks to develop analytical and expository skills. Reading assignments will enhance students' ability to contextualize and interpret evidence. Because discussion will play an important role in this course, it is important that students keep up with assignments and come prepared to engage in discussion. Writing assignments will hone students' proficiency in drafting clear, reasoned, and well-documented arguments.[4]

In addition to their substantive features, note in the preceding examples two stylistic ones. First, *diction*. To varying degrees, these syllabi employ not only abstractions, but also academic jargon. Students who haven't been initiated into literary analysis will be mystified by "fissures of textual effects." But a surprising number also won't understand "contextualize." Indeed, a senior honors student recently asked whether "expository problems" referred to his spelling. So take into account your audience. But again, I remind you that you're writing stage directions primarily to yourself, the director of the forthcoming fifteen-week academic drama.

Second, *voice*. In these statements of purpose, no one is speaking. By writing that "the course seeks to develop" for "students," the teacher has deleted his presence and depersonalized his audience. If you want an intellectual dialogue in your course, make the syllabus be part of it.

In the next two examples, the instructors use pronouns that signal a different relationship and thereby a clearer sense of what students are expected to do (and not do).

GENDER, COMMUNICATION, AND CULTURE

This course requires your active involvement. If you want to learn as much as possible, you should come to class ready to initiate ideas, share relevant experiences, reflect on what others say, and discuss and extend readings. Participating actively requires that you risk what you believe and how you define yourself—that you open yourself to other points of view and that you consider them critically. Rich discussion about gender and communication in our lives entails disagreements not only about issues, but also about basic values. As a member of this class you are expected to be respectful toward others and their views, even if those radically oppose your beliefs. If you are not willing to listen respectfully to others, you should drop this course.[5]

And here's an even more personalized voice:

CZECH 101

We will be getting our feet wet in Czech grammar and vocabulary this semester. Don't be afraid to wade in and soak up all you can. Please be sure to prepare for every class and bring in LOTS of questions. If at any time you begin to feel that you are falling behind, please inform the instructor immediately and come to office hours. The keys to success in this course are regular attendance and daily study. If you come to every class and do every assignment, I GUARANTEE you will do well in this course (and enjoy it too!). I have been doing this for a long time. Believe me. I know what works.[6]

Depending upon your values, you may also define your outcomes in terms that go *beyond* the classroom.

SOCIAL STATISTICS 141
The fundamental purpose of this course is to help you become what I would describe as a "conversant citizen." Each day, lawmakers, political commentators, teachers, and friends invoke the authority of U.S. census data and public opinion polls in an effort to sway your opinion on the issues of contemporary life. If you are to enter the debate with confidence, then you need to understand how the census and polls are designed, administered, used, and misused. With that knowledge, you'll be prepared to evaluate the arguments of others and to make your own independent judgments. Those are the essential skills of citizenship in a democratic society.[7]

En route toward your own statement of aims and outcomes, let's conclude with two examples that, in different styles, combine the ingredients we've been discussing.

After a paragraph summarizing several narrative themes, Barbara Harris outlines the concepts at work in her course:

HISTORY OF ENGLAND TO 1660
The goals of this course are:
   1. To provide you with a relatively coherent narrative and overview of English history to 1660;
   2. To introduce you to crucial categories of historical analysis such as gender, class, status, agency, ideology;
   3. To relate the specific material we are studying to fundamental

interpretative issues facing historians no matter what their sub-ject. Focusing on these issues will help you to organize what you are learning and to prepare for exams. Among the most important of these interpretive issues are:

    a. continuity versus change at what appear to be crucial turning points in history;

    b. the role of the individual in historical change;

    c. the causes of revolution;

    d. the ability of those without political or economic power to act as historical agents;

    e. the relationship between different kinds of social and political stratification (gender, class, status);

    4. To teach you how to read different kinds of primary sources, the materials out of which historians create their narratives about and interpretations of the past.[8]

At this point I suspect you're saying to yourself: "Four goals, five categories of analysis, and five issues, plus untold numbers of narrative themes! How in the world will I emulate that?" Once again let me reassure you that you won't and aren't expected to. Not the first time or even the third and fourth. Professor Harris herself arrived at this sophisticated definition only after thirty years of teaching and, more important, after consultation with the Center for Teaching and Learning on her campus. No one is a self-made teacher. All professors began learning their craft in graduate school. They continue to hone it by interchange with colleagues, perhaps with education consultants, and of course with their students. (In the bibliography, "If You Want to Learn More," you will find the websites of numerous Centers for Teaching and Learning.)

Two pieces of advice seem pertinent. First, be modest; you can't master every aspect of course design at once. Indeed, both you and your students will be newcomers, trying to master un-familiar material and skills in a few months. As I mentioned a few pages ago, rather than trying to accomplish everything, concen-trate on the two goals and skills that you consider most attainable and valuable.

Second, even as you solicit help from others, be yourself.

With that in mind, take heart from the opening paragraphs of a syllabus by a teacher fresh out of graduate school. He may not have ironed out every conceptual wrinkle, but his course description outlines his "promises" clearly. It defines what he will teach and also how students will learn. It states themes and also questions. And it does all this with the zest of a first-time tour guide.

UNITED STATES HISTORY SINCE 1865: INSIDERS AND OUTSIDERS
This course has the potential to be one of the most interesting and exciting you will take [in college]. The period we'll study, from 1865 to the 1980s, has seen technological, artistic, social, cultural, and political transformations that boggle the imagination. In this class we will survey some of these changes and try to make sense of their causes and consequences. We cannot cover everything worthy of our attention; some things have to be left out because there simply isn't enough time. So we're offering an intellectual buffet that allows you to sample from art, politics, architecture, war, literature, music, films, and folklore, and that introduces you to the wide range of material that makes up the American experience. We hope that you will continue in more specialized courses to pursue those subjects that interest you.

Given the wide-ranging nature of this course, how do we corral together Janis Joplin and Huey Long? Or *Playboy* and Reconstruction? To make sense of the long time period and the different materials, we've chosen a unifying theme that we call "insiders and outsiders." What does that mean? It means that we'll look closely at these questions:
- How and why have different people over time defined who is an American and who isn't?
- How and why has the American Dream differed according to the dreamer?
- Put simply, how and why do people and ideas get labeled as "American" or "un-American"?

Finally, we'll be exploring the three "R's": writing, reading, and reasoning. Historical writing and thinking [are] not restricted to a priestly caste. This course will help you hone the skills critical to thinking historically and to intelligently expressing your own understanding of the past. At the same time, you will learn how to apply these skills not just to the past, but to the future as well—both your own and America's.[9]

Before you leave this chapter, take a few minutes to brainstorm about the aims and outcomes in your course.

AIMS
- The main themes or ideas I will emphasize are _____.
- The big picture or story line is _____.
- The main questions I am interested in are _____.
- The mental model I am promoting is _____.

OUTCOMES
- To answer these questions, I want my students to become more skillful in doing _____.
- The mental model (paradigm of reality) that my students may bring with them and that I want to challenge is _____.

STYLE
- The diction and tone that I want to use are _____.

Practices

part Two

4 / Constructing a Syllabus

Having defined the destination of your course, you're ready to lay out the more specific "promises" that will take you and your students along the route. This chapter will help you construct a class-by-class calendar, including lectures, discussions, and reading and writing assignments—in sum, a "promising syllabus."

Most instructors who are designing a course—rookies as well as veterans—suffer from the obsession to "cover" everything. Behind this noble intention lurks the voice of the academic devil. In a survey of the English novel, for example, you can't imagine leaving out *Tom Jones, Vanity Fair*, and *Middlemarch*. Then again, can your students really read 2,280 pages in three weeks and also write that five-page midterm essay? In "U.S. History since 1945," you think you should spend a week on World War II, but looking ahead in the syllabus, how will you cover the Vietnam War in only one day? At moments like these, the devil whispers: "Don't worry. You can make the students read faster. You can lecture faster."

The truth is, however, that a speed-up strategy won't solve the problem. Large reading assignments and bell-to-bell, thickly detailed lectures tend to produce surface learning. *Less (material) equals more (learning)*.[1] This is not as paradoxical as it may first seem. Early-twentieth-century employers were astonished to find that when they reduced the workday from ten to eight hours, factory workers' productivity increased. The same principle holds true for students laboring in your course.

Even if you grudgingly let go of "coverage," however, you still have to figure out how to make those bedeviling decisions of what to exclude. There are no easy answers, and certainly not absolute ones. But I offer a four-step approach that will help you make your way through the quandary of coverage.

Material and time—these are your two antagonists. You will try to stuff too much material (topics, lectures, discussions, readings, exams) into too little time (so-and-so many weeks of so-and-so many classes). But exactly how much and how little? To measure what you're up against, I recommend the following tactics.

First, tape your statement of aims and outcomes above your desk where you won't lose sight of it. Let it serve as a generalized map to keep you on track as you plunge into the messy specifics.

Now take one of two paths, depending on whether you prefer to work inductively or deductively. Or if it suits you, commute between them.

For the *inductive* approach, begin by brainstorming all the topics that, ideally, you would include in your course, scribbling them onto a page in no particular order. That is, translate your general aims and themes into specifics. Better yet, scribble *questions*, because they are more powerful; questions engender topics.

Next, take out a calendar and list every class date, as well as every holiday, in the forthcoming semester.

Finally, match each question or topic with an available day of class. When you reach the last day you'll discover how many questions/topics remain "untaught." Coverage has collided with reality.

You can reach the same goal via a *deductive* path. Instead of inventing the questions/topics on your own, let the conventional authorities in your field do the job. For one thing, you should feel free and unapologetic to borrow from other professors' syllabi. Exchanging ideas is, after all, what scholars do. (You and I are doing it at this very moment in this book.) Also open a standard textbook in your field and list the title of every chapter or subchapter that, ideally, you want your students to know by the end of the course. Then pair each title (that is, topic) with a class day and discover by how much you have exceeded the time available.

Either way, inductively or deductively or some combination thereof, you will have charted an itinerary—unwieldy and impractical, but a start. Now you're ready for "uncoverage": that is, for deciding which topics to give up.

UNCOVERING

A scene from some long ago movie comes to mind. Fleeing his pursuers, the protagonist flings his clothes pell-mell into a suitcase, tries in vain to close the lid, and finally wields a pair of scissors to snip the sleeves and pant legs spilling over the edge. I presume you're looking for a selection process that is intellectually more defensible than this Suitcase Solution. I also presume you're wanting a course that has coherence and continuity.

First of all, I suggest that you *sequence* your provisional list of questions/topics according to your rationale for how the course will progress. Is your course chronological? Or does it build from basic principles to more sophisticated ones? Or does it go from theory to application, or vice versa? Whichever rationale you adopt, you also need to confront a big question: What do students need to know at this stage of the course, and what can be better addressed or understood later? Or even more important, what do they need to know at this stage in their intellectual journey through college? Your answer to these last two questions will help winnow topics that are interesting but unnecessary. (For a more detailed discussion, see the section below on "cognitive modulating.") Don't worry at this point about fine-tuning the transitions from one topic to the next. This is a rough draft.

Second, in order to define patterns among the questions/topics, *categorize* them according to which theme(s) they represent. And to make this process more graphic, color-code them. Like the English historian I quoted in chapter 3, you may be tracing gender (G-red), class (C-blue), status (S-green), agency (A-yellow) and ideology (I-black) across several centuries. Or, like an anthropologist of globalization, you may be emphasizing transnational migration, capital flows, and the like. When you're done, scan the list and take note of the distribution. Are most of the red questions/topics, for example, clustered in the first third of the course? Does this distribution match your intentions, or, on the contrary, does it signal that you forgot about this theme while planning the rest of the course? If the latter, you need to add questions/topics for this theme, even though that means you're lengthening a list that is already too long. But console yourself that you're improving the continuity and coherence.

Finally, you're ready to ponder which questions/topics, if push comes to shove, are dispensable. As a half-step, divide the list into four or five *units*, like chapters in a book. For historians, this is the process of periodization (the colonial era, the Revolution, the republic, etc.). A political science course may be moving not across time but across space: from local to state to federal. An introductory philosophy course may start with language before turning to ethics, aesthetics, and the mind-body problem. Even if you don't discern obvious dividing lines and "chapters," I encourage you to make rough cuts. One can't have second thoughts without risking some clumsy first thoughts. No revision without a prior vision.

As the next half-step, notice whether one unit is much longer than the others. It will be the first candidate for possible shrinkage. Engage in cold-blooded self-reflection. Why did you allocate disproportionate time to this section of your subject? Did you emphasize it because it's the most important? Or because you wrote your dissertation on it and feel underprepared to teach the other sections of your subject?

Even if you decide to pare this unit, however, you may nevertheless face that movie star's Suitcase Dilemma: more to pack than the calendar allows. Now comes the moment not only for reflection, but for ruthlessness. Which questions, topics, or themes can you delete and still have a course that fulfills the promise of its title? Which ones would your professional colleagues rank as indispensable or central to understanding the subject, and which ones peripheral?

Let me reassure you again: the first time you teach a course is inevitably a dress rehearsal. You will identify the excesses, omissions, and confusions only as you perform it in dialogue with a live audience.

Up to this point we have focused on you and your subject matter—the teacher and what will be taught. Now let's bring in the
third party to this relationship: the learners. As students pick up
your syllabus on the first day of class, they will want to know what
you will "cover" and why you care about it. More urgently, though,
they want to know what *they* will be expected to do.

- How many books or articles are there to read? Where are
  they obtainable?
- How many discussion sections, if any, will there be?
- How many exams, research papers, or Internet
  assignments are there, and of what length, and when are
  they due?
- How will grades be assigned?
- What is the attendance policy?

The more precisely you spell out what you expect students to do,
the more clearly they will understand how to succeed.

We will deal with writings and grading (plus attendance policies) in chapter 8. For the moment you need only think about
when to schedule writing assignments. The traditional model has
included a midterm, a final, and perhaps a research paper. Recently, however, many teachers have found that students learn
best by doing several writing assignments, short rather than long,
spread across the semester.[2] The reason is simple. If your students have trouble grasping the concepts or techniques in your
course, they (and you) need a second and third chance. Learning
improves with repetition.

Before nobly sprinkling the calendar with writing assignments, though, you need to think about your own workload. Three
blue-book exams times 60 students equals 180 exams, graded at,
say, 20 minutes apiece, equals 60 hours. A three-page research
paper for 60 students at 30 minutes apiece to grade equals another 30 hours. And that's not all. Repeat the arithmetic for the
other course(s) you'll be teaching. Pedagogy collides with exhaustion. There are no formulas for how much is too much to ask of
yourself. Assign what seems to make sense. And as we'll note in

Figure 4.1. Storyboard for a Syllabus

Unit 1: The Emergence of Modern Art, 1890–1914

Date	Question/Topic	Reading	Discussion	Writing
Jan. 12	Introduction What does "modern" mean?	No	No	No
Jan. 14	Impressionism Why was Cézanne crucial?	Textbook, chap. 1	No	No
Jan. 16	Cubism What is abstraction?	Articles 1–3	Yes	Reaction paper
Jan. 19	Picasso vs. Braque Collaborators or rivals?	Textbook, chaps. 2–3	No	Quiz
Jan. 21	Writing workshop How to use visual evidence?	No	Break-out groups	No
Jan. 23	Surrealism Why is surreal abstract?	No	No	First essay

chapter 8, you don't need to grade or even comment on every piece of writing.[3]

The same commonsense principle holds for readings. Students will fare best with shorter assignments at regular, frequent intervals—every week or two. Don't forget that your course is one of four or five that they're taking. While reading Mill's *On Liberty* for you, they may be reading Faulkner's *Absalom, Absalom,* plus studying three chapters of *Macroeconomics,* writing a research paper on abortion, and dissecting a frog.

Equally important, if you pair each reading with an opportunity for students to discuss it and/or write about it, they (and you) will know more effectively what they understood or have misunderstood.

By now you realize what has happened to your syllabus. After you struggled to define a list of topics and then struggled to shrink the list to fit the calendar, you have gone on to add exams and discussion sections, which means you have to delete more lectures. The challenge of "uncovering" does not relent. Moreover, you need to synchronize readings to lectures and discussions, and synchronize writing assignments to all three of those.

If you're feeling that you're juggling too many balls at once—or even if you're not feeling that way—try using what media people call a "storyboard" (see Figure 4.1). It will help you plot the relationships among the various components. Indeed, some teachers print their syllabus in a storyboard format because it furnishes students a clear overview of their responsibilities.

MODULATING

Besides meshing the activities of each week, a professor needs to calibrate the overall rhythm and sequence.[4] I have in mind not only the experiential dimension, but also the cognitive one.

Experiential Rhythm

People learn by repetition, but repetition can also turn into monotony. Break-out groups produce a welcome respite from the lecture mode, but after four break-out groups in four successive lectures, they will be predictable, routine, perhaps less lively. You may be the most scintillating teacher, but after thirty-one classes your students (as well as you) will welcome a different voice and approach. After all, the brain loves diversity. In addition, the spirit craves nourishment. As the semester builds toward its climax, students are falling behind, losing sleep to complete one or more term papers. In the fall semester they're succumbing to flu; in the spring semester, spring fever.

So I recommend that you build variations into the second half of your syllabus. Add one or two guest lecturers, for example. Perhaps schedule a film, a debate, a simulation, or a field trip (see chapter 7). You would also do well to list one day as TBA (to be announced)—in case you proceed more slowly than expected or have to cancel a class because of an ice storm or your daughter's strep throat.

Cognitive Sequence

In addition to varying the experiential rhythm, you need to pay attention to how you design the cognitive sequence. People learn best by starting with simple material before confronting complexity. Regular verbs before irregular ones. Simple equations before quadratic ones. James Joyce's *Dubliners* before *Ulysses*. This principle is hardly surprising; indeed, it's commonsensical. Putting it into practice, however, proves surprisingly tricky.

Unlike the sciences, mathematics, economics, and foreign languages, knowledge in the humanities isn't necessarily structured cumulatively.[5] Therefore, teachers of history, literature, and philosophy don't always arrange a syllabus in order of difficulty. A so-called introductory course like Western Civilization, for example, begins not with conjugating the verb *"parler"* or solving $2x + 4 = 13$, but with reading Plato. That's like plunging novice whitewater rafters into level five rapids. How can a professor successfully guide first-year students through *The Republic* when most of them still think history consists of memorizing facts and dates?

The quantitative solution seems obvious enough: assign less

and proceed more slowly than you would later in the semester, when students have become better-trained historians. On second thought, though, this solution sidesteps the basic problem. *The Republic* doesn't necessarily prepare students to understand Augustine's *Confessions* and, in turn, Machiavelli's *The Prince*. These texts don't form building blocks from simple to complex or regular to irregular. They move laterally to other authors and subjects that present fresh complexities.

To build a cumulative curriculum, you should plan not simply the content, but what you want students *to do* with the content— that is, *cognitive skills*. We're returning to the aims and outcomes (chapter 3). If you're like most professors, you have defined your aims in general terms: "think critically; interpret evidence; hone an argument." These work well enough to chart your goals, but they don't address the specific steps by which beginners will learn how to critique, interpret, or hone. This omission isn't surprising. After all, professors used to be those undergraduate students who leapfrogged the rudimentary steps. That's how they became professors. To teach slower students, professors must back up, slowly analyze their mental processes, and explicate the intermediate steps they have taken for granted.

For example, if you pose that favorite graduate seminar question, "what is the main flaw in Malinowski's argument?" you're presuming that your undergraduates already comprehend his argument. A lecture on the "structure" of Van Gogh's landscape presumes that students will know how to overlook the scenery and see the painting in formal terms.

As with everything else about teaching, these issues will be solved most effectively in the crucible of classroom practice. You'll figure out how to set appropriate cognitive expectations through the dialogic back-and-forth with your students. If someone in the front row raises her hand and asks, "What do you mean by 'structure'?" you'll hear the signal to back up and fill in the missing steps of analysis.

In the meantime, though, Benjamin Bloom's classic ladder of cognitive skills may prove enlightening. Usually, a student needs to work successfully on the lower rungs before climbing to the higher ones. As you devise lectures, frame discussions, or formulate exam questions, ask yourself which type of cognitive skill you're asking students to perform:

1. *Recall*—A student remembers factual materials; verbs that a teacher uses include *define, describe, list, name, identify.*
2. *Understand*—A student grasps the meaning of a concept; verbs include *put in your own words, discuss, explain, classify.*
3. *Apply*—A student is asked to solve problems; verbs include *apply, illustrate, demonstrate, use.*
4. *Analyze*—A student understands the structure and components; verbs include *analyze, compare, contrast, criticize, examine.*
5. *Synthesize*—A student combines ideas to form a new whole; verbs include *compose, create, design, formulate.*
6. *Evaluate*—A student is asked to make value judgments; verbs include *appraise, argue, assess, support, attack, recommend.*[6]

If this six-step model seems bewilderingly complicated (as I've found to be true for many new teachers), here is a simplified three-step version:

1. *Knowing*—A student has the ability to memorize, comprehend, and express ideas in one's own words.
2. *Understanding*—A student recognizes examples and sees relationships.
3. *Thinking*—A student applies what he/she has learned, creating something beyond what exists.[7]

In the early weeks of the course, you should keep your eye on lower-level skills while working your students toward the more interesting, sophisticated issues. Unless they know the meaning of a concept like "structure," and can express it in their own words, they won't be able to analyze it in Van Gogh's paintings or compare Van Gogh's structure to Braque's. I am not advocating recitation drills, though. Ideally, students will come to learn the concepts *in the context of* grappling with issues that captivate them. Think of learning to play the piano. True, students must practice their scales, but they will become quickly discouraged if they don't have

Figure 4.2. Heading for a Syllabus

POLI 101: Introduction to Political Science
Prof. Jessica Smith   Class meets at
Office: 417 Newlands Hall   Hamilton Hall 102
Office hours, Tues. & Fri., 2–4, &   MWF 9:00 A.M.
by appointment
902-0987; jsmith@email.edu
(Home, 877-7654—before 10 P.M., please)

---

the chance to play real songs, even if only simple tunes like "Myr-
tle the Turtle." When your students first tackle sophisticated problems, their use of fundamental concepts may sound woefully
heavy-handed and off-key, but you're helping them on the way
toward playing intellectual sonatas. Even in mathematically oriented fields like economics, many outstanding teachers help students grasp advanced concepts by engaging them in problems
long before conventional wisdom says that they know enough.

Easier said than done, especially if your students are a mix of
novices and majors in your field. Gauging the right pitch will also
be difficult if you're starting out at a university where you're un-
familiar with the students' abilities. Again, let me reassure you:
trial and error will be your best teacher. If you discover, a few
weeks into your course, that students aren't "getting" something,
consult these cognitive models and reflect on whether you've set
the mental task at too high a level. If they're impatient, move
higher on the ladder.

After so much attention to gauging students' attitudes and
abilities, you may be clucking, "Standards! What about standards!" That is, you may think that my approach advocates satisfy-
ing every student at the price of diluting quality and difficulty. On
the contrary, it wants to help you maintain high standards by
enabling students to reach them. I'm not addressing the content
of your course. I'm addressing the process by which you teach
them to grasp the content.[8]

Now comes the easy part of constructing a syllabus. At the top of the first page, list the basic information that your students will need to know (see Figure 4.2):

- What is the course name and number?
- Where and when does the class meet?
- Who are you?
- How can they find you? (Note your office location and office hours, e-mail address, and office telephone number; you may also choose to list your home phone number, with a limit such as "Don't call after 10:00 P.M.")

After the section on "Aims and Outcomes," and either before or after the calendar,

- list the books to be purchased and materials to be read on reserve at the library;
- outline the grading system (what proportion of 100 percent will you give to each assignment?).[9]

How long is a typical syllabus? I have seen ones as short as two pages and as long as twenty or more. As Voltaire remarked, he would have written a shorter letter if he had more fully understood what he had in mind. Likewise, your syllabus may shrink in future years as you become a more experienced course designer. In any event, informativeness, not length, is the relevant criterion. In however many pages one requires, a "promising" syllabus should define:

1. *The promise*—What you will "cover" and what your students will learn to do better (understand more clearly, solve problems, etc.).
2. *Means toward the promise*—How you and your students will work to realize these goals. (This is conventionally called the "requirements.")
3. *Measurement of progress*—How you and your students will understand how much of the promise has been realized. (This is conventionally called "grading.")

5 / Lecturing

If you eavesdrop on college classrooms, odds are that the voice you hear will be the professor's. According to a 1987 study of undergraduate liberal arts programs at more than eighty universities, lecturing was the instructional method in 81 percent of social science courses, 89 percent of physical sciences and mathematics courses, and (astonishingly) 90 percent of philosophy courses.[1] Lecturing is the prevalent modus operandi for good reasons and for not-so-good ones.

On the positive side, lectures work as effectively as other methods to deliver information and ideas. On the negative side, they work less effectively than discussion for promoting independent thought or developing cognitive skills.[2] Given this limitation, critics will ask, "Why not scan the text onto the course Web page or videotape the lecture, and use class time for more interactive learning?" But that misses another positive aspect of lecturing. Unlike a book or even a videotape, a lecturer has live, face-to-face contact with students. In other words, he/she provides a *relationship*, an experience shared among a large group. (Contrast the experience of watching a film in a movie house with watching it on the vcr in one's living room.) Accordingly, students rate "good" lecture experiences as ones that involved them not only via the ideas, but via the teacher as a person—his/her tone, commitment, and enthusiasm. They give "bad" ratings to lectures that entailed only ideas.[3]

There are also pragmatic reasons for lecturing. The most obvious is cost-efficiency: how else can one instructor teach several hundred students? Likewise, most professors talk their way through a course for reasons of pedagogical efficiency. How else, they say, can I "cover" all this material and deliver it to all these students? (The next chapter will offer several answers to these apparently irrefutable rhetorical questions.)

New teachers are particularly drawn to lecturing because they're still mastering the material. That is, they're learning it for themselves and not yet able to redefine it into step-by-step learning for students. It's like playing a sport or visiting a foreign country for the first time. Only gradually does one grasp the underlying principles, much less invent ways to help other people discover them.

Unfortunately, some evidence suggests that lecturers are wasting much of their talent and energy. When tested immediately after leaving a lecture, students recall, on average, 40 percent of the information. Worse, most of what they recall comes from the first ten minutes.[4] Between "delivery" of the lecture and its reception falls an ominous pedagogical shadow. Students learn more when they're active rather than passive.

Nevertheless, lecturing remains the staple of college teaching. Given that fact, how can you outflank its inherent limitations, even in classes of one hundred students or more? This chapter offers tried-and-true techniques for designing lectures that will hold students' attention and maximize their comprehension. Chapter 7 will offer ways of going beyond this traditional format altogether.

Let's begin with the recipe for the kind of lecture that gives lectures a bad name. As the bell rings, Professor X scans his notes and waits for the 150 students to quiet down. "Today's topic is the religious beliefs and practices of the Balinese," he says, launching into the first of the eight points listed on the overhead transparency, explaining *bayu*, *balian*, and *banjar*, speaking more and more rapidly as the minute hand approaches the fifty-minute mark, trying to cover the final two points, only to announce at the bell, "I'll finish up on Wednesday." Unfortunately, despite all his hard work, Professor X has not made the best use of this teaching occasion. *Knowing*, *understanding* and *thinking*: these are the cognitive levels mentioned in chapter 4. Even the most interested students will hold in mind (know) only a fraction of the eight-point information as they go off to chem lab or chat on their cell phones. Most students wrote copious notes, but Professor X allowed them little time to understand his ideas, much less to think about them. By the end of class, they were probably feeling overwhelmed, hence bewildered or bored.

How can you develop a lecture that will successfully engage your audience? As Ken Bain discovered in his study of outstanding teachers, both lecturers and non-lecturers employed the same set of techniques in their classes.[5]

FIVE KEYS TO SUCCESS

(1) Pose a question, either at the beginning or partway through the lecture. For example, "Why do the Balinese regard death with seeming lightheartedness?"

To dramatize the question, you can embed it in a *vignette*. Find a quotation, an anecdote, a photograph, or some other type of vivid material that crystallizes the issue you'll be exploring in the next hour. Professor X can read an eyewitness account of the whirling, undulating procession of mourners, accompanied by an orchestra of drums, xylophones, and cymbals, en route to the cremation grounds. A sociologist may open a lecture on class and gender by reporting that Jack Welch, former chief executive officer of General Electric, earned in one day as much as the woman caring for his child at a day-care center earned in one year. A literature professor may preface a discussion of "The Wasteland" by playing a tape of Eliot reading the poem.

A vignette does more than grab attention. As noted in chapter 2, students have different learning preferences. A large number of them understand more easily via sensory examples because their minds move inductively, from particular evidence toward general, abstract concepts.[6]

(2) But how will you satisfy those other students who work best by starting with general, abstract concepts? Either before or after the vignette, state (and write on the board) the *significance* of the question for the day. For example, help your students understand

how the question relates to some larger question. ("I'm using the Balinese cremation ceremonies as a case study to illustrate the ethic of relatedness that we discussed last week.")

You may state the significance in impersonal terms. But you'll have more impact if you convey your own curiosity or passion. Tell your students what is at stake—the "so what" underlying the topic you've chosen. Try to make them care as much as you do. One of the problems we face as teaching scholars is that we're interested in certain questions because we were once interested in earlier questions, which intrigued us because of even earlier questions. Don't forget that our students have not yet taken that intellectual journey. While we are digging deep underground at rich intellectual ore, they are standing on the surface wondering why anyone in his right mind would be engaged in that subterranean expedition.[7]

(3) The best teachers go beyond simply "remember this." For example, they compare two schools of thought on a subject. Or they work with evidence, analyzing and evaluating it, unfolding an interpretation, modeling how an anthropologist (philosopher, historian, etc.) works.

(4) Offer your own answer, complete with evidence and conclusions. In other words, you are demonstrating the best way to deal with the question of the day. In some cases, this might take up most of the class hour, but it is embedded in a larger, hence more meaningful context.

(5) Leave students with a question.

These five techniques don't add up to a foolproof or professor-proof recipe, but I'm confident that they will serve you well. Nevertheless, to construct and deliver a varied, dramatic lecture is only one part of the process. You also want your students to *receive* it.

Effective lecturing, like all forms of teaching, is dialogic. That holds true even when one person is talking and one hundred are listening. Ideally, the listeners will be responding silently in their minds and in their notebooks. In reality, attention dips and wanders sporadically throughout the hour. How can a teacher maximize the chances of being listened to?

First of all, please note: you don't have to be brilliant. You needn't write lectures that emulate the essays that impressed your professors in graduate school. Indeed, as I mentioned earlier, brilliance (that subterranean digging) will likely be counterproductive. It may dazzle you but leave your students with drooping eyelids. Nor will you have time to write trailblazing lectures for every class. For your sake and your students' sake, then, push aside the scholarly monographs. Instead, open three textbooks or general sources (other than the one you've assigned) and spend no more than three or four hours cobbling their information into your interpretation. This process sounds crass, but as almost every new teacher has testified, it's the best technique to keep pace during your first year.

Let me quickly emphasize that I'm not recommending merely a textbook pastiche.[8] That would be a recipe for ineffective teaching. To engage your students in a teaching/learning dialogue, you should add two crucial ingredients: *question(s)* and *significance* ("so what"). You thereby transform information into a search for meanings.

If original ideas are not the key to effective teaching, what is? According to every research study, undergraduates rank highest those lecturers who are enthusiastic and organized. But what exactly do these two qualities mean in classroom practice, and how does one acquire them?

ENTHUSIASM

If you are introverted, shy, or soft-spoken, enthusiasm may not come easily. Don't worry. By adopting a few techniques, you will convey a sense of enthusiasm to your students.

At the top of the list is a resounding negative: Don't read your lecture. No matter how lively the ideas on the page, they will lose their vitality if you read them. For one thing, only the most theatrical instructors can escape slipping into a drone. Moreover, by looking down at the page and staying rooted behind the lectern, you forfeit eye contact with your listeners. As a result, they can't read your face to supplement your words. And you can't receive their nonverbal cues (smiles, yawns, heads shaking "no" or nodding "yes"). Especially if you're not the demonstrative type, you need to rely on supplementary modes of expressing your ideas and expressing yourself as the teacher of those ideas.

Think of your classroom as a theater and your role as an actor.[9] Before class, don't simply review your lecture notes (script); define the feelings that you attach to your ideas. When you start class (raise the curtain), you will thereby set an atmosphere and focus the audience's attention. Begin by saying something along the lines of "I find today's topic interesting (fascinating, exciting) because . . . ." During the hour, use not only your voice but also your body. Make eye contact. Use gestures to underline your ideas. Move to different sides of the stage and walk up the aisles.

Keep in mind: an essay and a lecture are as different as writing and speaking. (Imagine having a conversation with someone who reads his responses aloud to you.) In contrast to a well-crafted piece of writing, a lecture should employ a simpler overall structure ("the second cause of . . .") and simpler sentences. Periodic rephrasing ("in other words . . ."; "as an analogy, think of . . .") and planned silences will allow the ideas to sink in.[10]

ORGANIZATION

As a way to organize effective lectures, you may (if you are a visual learner) find useful the chart in Figure 5.1.

Undergraduates typically can absorb no more than two or perhaps three new ideas in a single session. Moreover, their attention sags halfway through the hour.[11] It's good practice, therefore, to divide your lecture into two parts—two main ideas, themes, or issues. (See the second column of the chart.)

Halfway through, take a long breath (or maybe two or three breaths). Before launching into Idea 2, you will benefit your students and yourself by interjecting a pause—like a bench beside the mountain trail that allows the hiker to appreciate what he/she has accomplished thus far. Silence also teaches.

All of this may sound daunting. Let me assure you that it soon

Figure 5.1. Constructing a Lecture

Time	Content	Activity	Resource
0–5 minutes	Question; vignette		
6–25	Idea 1	Lecture	Slides
26–30	Reflect	Break-out group; 60-second essay	
31–45	Idea 2	Lecture; debate and vote	Video clip; ballots
46–50	Wrap-up; question		

Source: Adapted from Greg Light and Roy Cox, *Learning and Teaching in Higher Education: The Reflective Professional* (London: Sage Publications, 2001), 110, reproduced by permission of Sage Publications Ltd.

becomes second nature. After a few weeks, you'll structure your lectures automatically. And in the classroom, you'll eventually proceed with barely a glance at the clock.

Organization is a sine qua non, but the best lecturers add variety and drama. Indeed, students these days have grown up expecting—or even demanding—more than a "talking head." They spend hours a day amid the blitz of media, cell-phoning, instant messaging, listening to CDs, and watching fourway-split-screen television newscasts, often doing more than one of these simultaneously. To be sure, you are a teacher, not an entertainer. Still, what else can you do besides including an opening vignette to enhance your ideas with variety and drama? There are as many possibilities as your imagination can conjure and one or other media can produce. Consider, for example, the following activities or resources (columns 3 and 4 in Figure 5.1) to enliven your lecture.

(1) *Visualizing:* Whenever possible, use some sort of visual accompaniment. People learn better via more than one sensory channel. Head-shots of Ho Chi Minh and Diem, for instance,

help students differentiate North from South Vietnam. A photograph of a runaway slave's back scarred by brutal whipping speaks unforgettably for itself. Without a map, you'll have enormous difficulty discussing the Israeli-Palestinian conflict. You may rattle off statistics about birthrates as students frantically scribble them down or plead "can you repeat that?"; a graph does the job more efficiently. Better yet, also include in your syllabus or course Web page the Web addresses for these sources, so students can download them for further analysis.

(2) *Hearing*: To avoid the monotony of a single voice (namely, yours), you can hand out copies of the quotations in your lectures to student volunteers and, at appropriate moments, have them read the words aloud. The effect is usually enlivening, sometimes delightful. I recall an otherwise soft-spoken young woman who declaimed a fiery manifesto by a nineteenth-century anarchist. You can also employ PowerPoint slides, videotape, or CDs. Think twice, though. Each of these requires time and equipment that you may not have. More important, technology is only a means toward learning. Indeed, if you create too high-powered a presentation, you may make your students passive.

(3) *Reflecting*: Silence is also a teacher. Some lecturers pause en route to ask, "Is there anything I need to clarify?" The question typically evokes nothing but silence because few students want to seem "dumb," especially before a crowd of their peers. Or else someone asks, "How do you spell Spinoza?"

You can use silence more effectively by turning it into activity. Between Idea 1 and Idea 2, ask students to "hold a discussion with yourself by writing what you've learned thus far." After a minute of scribbling, they not only will assimilate what they understand, but they will realize what they don't understand. Now they will ask more substantive questions than "how do you spell Spinoza?" Alternatively, if no one speaks up, you can ask for a volunteer to state the main point of the past half hour.

To exploit even more fully this pause for reflection, you might sometimes add two short and enormously productive steps to the reflective process. Let's call this technique "Think—Pair—Share."

1. *Think*—Pose a question either as review ("What has been the main point so far?" "Why do the Balinese regard death lightheartedly?") or as transition to Idea 2 ("Given what you've heard, . . . ?") Give them sixty seconds to write an answer.

2. *Pair*—Tell students to confer with a neighbor (for two or maybe five minutes) and compare answers.

3. *Share*—Ask one pair to report their answer. Ask whether other pairs have different answers. After a brief discussion, move on to Idea 2.

At this point you may be muttering, "With only fifty minutes I have precious little time to teach, so why should I spend five or ten of them in this maneuver?" Here's an answer. If teachers talk six minutes less, our students recall more! That is the counterintuitive and humbling conclusion of an empirical study of several courses. A lecturer paused for two minutes at three separate junctures during the hour. At each pause, students conferred in pairs. In the last few minutes of the lecture, students wrote down everything they recalled. Two weeks later, when given a multiple-choice test, they scored two letter grades better than a control group that had sat through a lecture without pauses.[12]

Again, silence is a teacher, even (or especially) in a lecture.

Employ the five keys to success. Define two main themes, plus a vignette and a conclusion. Organize and be enthusiastic. Insert audiovisual dramatization. Speak and be silent.

It may seem an impossible prescription unless you remind yourself that lecturing, like any interesting skill, develops gradually. That eloquent, riveting professor whom you wish to emulate was once a shaky-voiced novice clutching his or her notes. If you concentrate first on organization and clarity, your students will learn effectively. The rest will come with practice.

6 / Discussing

In your graduate program, you may have served as a teaching assistant and learned to facilitate discussions by small groups. What you probably haven't done, however, is synchronize small-group discussions with other parts of a course. Ideally, discussions, lectures, readings, and writing assignments each play their complementary part in the symphony of learning. So you, the composer and then conductor, need to write the score for that chorus of voices.

You can't begin working out these logistics, though, before deciding where you want to go and why you want to go there. (As you may notice, we're repeating the self-reflective sequence of chapters 1 through 3.)

DEFINING AIMS AND RATIONALES

Let's begin with a disconcertingly basic question: Why hold discussions at all? Certain types of students (and you may have been one of them) find little value in hearing their classmates exchange ideas. Shy people tremble at the prospect of being asked to speak in front of others. Introverts, who process their thoughts before speaking, resent competing with those who "shoot their mouths off." More important, rather than waste their time in this intellectual democracy, they prefer to hear from the professor (the expert) and to think on their own.

For the majority of undergraduates, on the other hand, discussion sections of fifteen to twenty students provide a welcome alternative to the large class as a whole. They can enjoy a less intimidating, more personal setting—a place where, to quote the theme song of the television series *Cheers*, everyone knows your name. As mentioned in chapter 2, most undergraduates prefer to learn in collaboration with others.

But learn what? Peel off the familiar label "discussion," and you'll discover that it conceals at least three, quite distinctive kinds of learning. In a *recitation*, the teacher asks closed-ended questions, and the students provide right answers (or wrong ones). In other words, you pitch the baseball, and they try to hit it. A recitation works well if you want to help students comprehend (that is, put in their own words) last week's lecture or today's reading, or to help them prepare for an upcoming exam.

TEACHER: According to the author, what is the main defect of federal deficits?

STUDENT: They increase the amount of interest the government has to pay on the debt.

TEACHER: And how is that significant?

STUDENT: It limits spending on other non-entitlement budget items.

TEACHER: Yes, that is the short-run significance. What about longer-run consequences?

In a *conversation*, by contrast, you don't bring a fixed agenda other than to induce a lively, fruitful exploration of the day's topic. Instead of handling the ball of conversation after each student speaks, you watch it being bounced like a beach ball among a rock concert crowd and wait for your turn. Because this kind of discussion is more open-ended and spontaneous, it works well to arouse energy and to bring in timid students. Sometimes it will be lighthearted, sometimes intense. Either way, consider holding a conversation for part of the class hour. As the following vignette illustrates, personalized discussion may lead to powerful outcomes.

I had devised a pedagogical strategy for my small-group discussion of the Vietnam War, starting with open-ended questions ("What surprised you?") and moving on to analytic issues ("How does Herr's description of the battle of Khe Sanh differ from the *Washington Post*'s account?"). Michael Herr's *Dispatches* was more journalism than history: subjective, evocative, novelistic memoir, filled with sounds and smells and drugs, obscenities, raw fear, crazed rock-and-roll cadences. Ten minutes into the discussion, I asked: "What was the most compelling part of the book for you?" A student named Pam said in a tremulous voice: "I feel guilty." Interesting, I thought, that she would confess to not having done the reading.

But that was not what she was saying. "My father served in Vietnam," she continued, "but he never talked about it." She took a shaky breath. "Not to my mom, or my sister, or me. In all these years not a word." She held the book to her chest. "But now I know what he must have gone through and I feel guilty that I know." Tears were trickling down her face.

The room was quiet. Several students were nodding in agreement. Someone handed Pam a tissue. I murmured some words of commiseration, stunned by her confession.

Another student leaned forward. "I know what you mean. My dad was over there too, and he won't ever say anything. When I go home I'm going to tell him about this book and ask him questions."

Amy raised her hand and opened her mouth to speak, but at first all she could do was sob soundlessly. "I feel so bad for my dad," she said finally. "Now I understand how awful it must have been for him in Vietnam." She pressed the back of her hand against her tears. "And he was younger than I am."

Early in the semester I had proclaimed facilely: "We are part of history and, whether you realize it or not, history is part of us." Now that epigram came to life in unexpected form. Somehow I hadn't realized that the war was now so long ago that it had spawned a new generation, children of the vets. I had read countless books and seen (or avoided) numerous films about the war, so I had forgotten that many students were encountering the saga for the first time and were freshly susceptible to the horrors. I had focused on the history of the war but had overlooked the history of my students. They taught me that each generation not only carries a different past into the classroom but also brings the secrets of their fathers.[1]

Midway along the continuum between these two models is a kind of discussion that I call a *seminar*. You are aiming for a more substantive and probing analysis of the day's topic than in a conversation. And instead of a recitation's predetermined answers, you bring a few issues and perspectives that will challenge students' thinking. To reach that goal, you serve as a facilitator, intervening when the ball of conversation rolls out of bounds or loses air. Of course, you should also exercise your authority, seizing occasions to provide insights and crystallize the issues under discussion.

In college in my first philosophy course I had a marvelous teacher, one of the great ones. . . . One day toward the end of the year, we were discussing a particularly boring text. I don't remember the author or the text or the issue we were discussing. But it was a beautiful spring day; the class had not prepared very well and the discussion was desultory. At one point the teacher asked a question; a student eventually raised his hand and gave an answer. The teacher turned to another student and asked her what she thought of the answer. She replied that she thought it was wrong and she gave another, quite different answer. There was a silence—it went on for a while and everybody began to get a little uneasy. The teacher turned to the class. "Well?" he said in a questioning tone. More silence and uneasiness. What was he asking? What was he doing? What did he want? Suddenly, he picked up his book and slammed it down very loudly on the table. "Damn it all," he said, "you've just heard two diametrically opposed answers to the same question. They can't both be right. At least one of them must be wrong. After all, it does make a difference!" For me, that last remark was like a bolt of lightning. He was right; it did make a difference! That may have been the moment at which I decided to study philosophy.[2]

I'm not endorsing one of these three alternatives to the exclusion of the others. Each carries a certain intellectual benefit and advantage. The point is that you should decide which one suits your purposes in a given class. Or, more likely, you may wish to mix them. For example, you may believe that discussion should begin with efforts to answer interpretive questions about a text (seminar), reserving comprehension (recitation) and judgment questions (conversation) for the end.[3] On the other hand, I prefer to open with a conversational gambit ("What surprised you?" or "If you were U.S. president in 1861 . . ." or "Quote your favorite sentence . . .") because students will then be engaged in solving problems that *they* regard as important or intriguing.[4] Whatever your plan, explicate it to yourself . . . and also to your students. Remember that they bring to the classroom their mental models of what is supposed to happen. So you need to tell them which model you have chosen and how you want them to participate— the rules of the ball game.

Having said all this, however, we still haven't answered that disconcertingly basic question: Why discuss? For a recitation the rationale is obvious: it serves as an oral quiz, ensuring that students have understood their homework, a lecture, and/or the material for an upcoming exam. But why schedule a more open-ended seminar or conversation and, more to the point, why expect students to participate?

Let's begin with a *pedagogical* justification. When students speak, they feel more personally invested and take away more. Duke University professor Anne Scott once asked her seminar, "Who remembers what we were talking about last week?" A student raised his hand. "I don't remember what you were saying, but I remember what I said." Yes, that's the number-one benefit of discussion: students learn more when they are active rather than passive. In addition, they gain by sharing the give-and-take that marks intellectual and emotional learning. That process isn't learned at a distance, any more than playing tennis or using a computer is learned by watching someone do it. Only in a small group can students acquire the hands-on experience. It can be a significant experience. Do you remember how you felt when you first walked into your own classroom: a fluttery stomach but also the thrill of authority? Providing students an opportunity to discuss gives them a taste of that self-assertion.

Besides this pedagogical justification for discussing, I also offer a *civic* one. If the best teaching is dialogic, then our students ought to perform their share. Simply showing up and taking notes doesn't fulfill their responsibility. Citizenship in the republic of ideas calls for more active involvement. Each student needs to put his or her ideas into the forum, deal with classmates' questions or challenges, and work toward the collective good. Like democracy, discussion affords a space for all views in order to promote human development.[5] Indeed, this experience should help your students carry on thoughtful conversations outside of class.

Here is how a teaching assistant eloquently expressed this rationale:

For me, the discussion section is a place for students to be active participants in a community of learning. I strive to strike a balance between conveying information, honing analytical skills, and facilitating teamwork. I de-emphasize grades and I stress mastery and collaboration. My role is to provide students with the encouragement and the training they need in order to find and evaluate information, lead their own discussions, problem-solve, ask challenging questions, and be self-motivated learners.[6]

Students, on the other hand, may expect to play a significantly different role. More than likely, they see themselves not as citizens but as consumers, who have paid tuition to earn 120 hours of credit in as efficient and gratifying a fashion as possible. So they may want to sit back rather than jump in. They may want to leave the classroom with pages of orderly notes rather than a head filled with ambiguous, nonlinear ideas. They may want answers—"the truth"—rather than interpretations.

Let's not blame them for this mode of thinking. Their high schools encouraged it by setting up hurdles of standardized end-of-year tests. Colleges reinforce it by asking students to navigate a maze of required and elective courses. Some of your colleagues, lecturing nonstop at one hundred words per minute and issuing pop quizzes, will further reinforce it. Your students arrive in your classroom not as tabula rasa, but as individuals who probably have been playing (and succeeding) by rules that conflict with yours. So you need to tell them, loudly and clearly, in the syllabus, on the first day, and before every discussion meeting, what you expect of them.

As you read excerpts from the following three syllabi, reflect upon which one most closely matches the expectations and tone that you want to communicate.

The discussions, which are scheduled for the end of the week, provide a forum for dealing with questions raised by the readings and the lectures and for preparing for papers and exams. Discussion attendance is a required, not an optional part of the course. Reflecting the importance of discussion sessions, 20 percent of the course grade will be assigned on the basis of attendance and participation. Participating in a group discussion is important both as a skill and as a learning opportunity. However, not all students are equally comfortable with the process. Those feeling ill at ease should at the very beginning of the term ask their discussion leader's help on techniques for getting into the flow of the discussion.[7]

Regarding the discussion sections, a couple of points are worth spelling out. First, this course is organized on the conviction that nobody (including your professor and TA) knows everything, but that everybody knows and can contribute something. No scholar could write or teach anything without the work of other scholars. In the same way, group discussion clarifies the course material more fully than any student could do alone. Second, professors have also learned that questions are usually more illuminating than answers. Every question asked in discussion (or lecture) is on the minds of more students than just the one asking it, so you should never hesitate to ask a question. Asking a question invariably implies interest, which implies knowledge. Your questions will be regarded as contributions to discussion and will be rewarded accordingly.[8]

Students are permitted two unexcused absences (the equivalent of one week) in lecture. These absences MUST NOT BE DURING THE FOUR DISCUSSION SESSIONS. After that, students lose one-third letter grade for each absence. I will accept a formal excuse from the Dean of Students, student health services, or other health care professional, but auto-excuses (ones you give yourself) are not acceptable even if you did sleep through your alarm clock, got delayed by traffic, suffered a broken heart, etc.

Students must write four two-to-three-page TYPED papers, based on the four monographs, which answer the assigned questions. We will break up into four sections to discuss these papers. Twenty percent of your paper grade will be based on your participation in discussion. The TA's will grade contributions to discussions by quality, not quantity, and no student will be permitted to monopolize discussion. Nor will students be permitted to remain silent.[9]

SUCCEEDING

If a lecture produces more learning when students do more than listen and take notes, this principle holds even truer for a discussion. Whether staging a recitation, conversation, or seminar, teachers want their classrooms to reverberate with many voices.

"How will I make that happen?" you ask. The first answer is that you won't and can't make a discussion succeed, not by yourself. You and your students together will make it (or break it). As a rough analogy, think of a basketball coach who calls out plays and shouts encouragement from the bench but otherwise depends on his or her players to win the game.

The second answer shifts from the actual discussion to two phases of preparation for it. The better you lay the groundwork, the more likely you'll enjoy a successful outcome. Months beforehand, you will select the particular readings and think about how they resonate with your lectures and other readings. A week beforehand, you (and your TAS, if you have them) will figure out how to convey your aims to the students. By the time that you and your fifteen students take seats in the classroom, you will have already completed most of your job as discussion leader.

Before the Course Begins

If you're like most professors, you intend to hold a series of small-group discussions around various books or articles. In deciding when and how often to schedule them, ask yourself: Are the assignments spread fairly evenly across the semester? Does the topic of each reading pertain to the lectures before and after?

But a course is more than a sequence of topics. You're choreographing an *experience* that you and your students will share during several months. As you construct the calendar, you also need to imagine how it will function and evolve from class to class, week to week. By meeting in small groups, you and your students become more familiar with one another. As the literal distance shrinks, so does the psychological. People will learn names, feel recognized, relax. When the large class reconvenes, you won't be addressing a sea of anonymous faces, nor will students feel themselves among a crowd of strangers. As a result, they will be more willing to raise questions and participate in break-out sessions. The bonds of a learning community will be growing.

The sooner you start this process, the less inertia you will need to overcome. First impressions are crucial. Whatever you do at the outset will largely determine student behavior throughout the semester. On the first day, make sure that students talk at least briefly. You might, for example, tell each student to exchange introductions with a neighbor, saying name, birthplace, and favorite nonacademic activity (or the best thing that happened to them this week). After you introduce yourself, ask students to name people or issues they expect to study in this course. Here you elicit their mental model (or stereotypes).[10] For the same reason, you would also do well to schedule the first small-group discussion early in the semester, and then reinforce the process with a second discussion soon afterward. From then on, small-group meetings at regular intervals (every week or two) will sustain the sense that you and your students are working together in two overlapping settings, small and large, a neighborhood within the city.

Even though you want to schedule discussions early and evenly, keep an eye out for logjams. Have you given students enough time to do the assignment? If the discussion comes immediately before or after an exam or paper, for instance, they will feel overloaded and resentful. Equally important, have you given *yourself* enough time? You don't want to be planning and guiding discussions while feverishly grading sixty exams.

Finally, you may also need to solve a logistical dilemma. In the ideal Platonic world a teacher meets with fifteen students every week, but modern academia tends, alas, to be quite unplatonic. What if your course contains sixty students and you have no TAS? Here are several solutions, all of them imperfect.

You can form three, twenty-person groups; schedule one of them at the class hour (for example, Fridays at 11:00 A.M.), and schedule the other two at hours when those students are able to meet (for example, Fridays at 8:00 A.M. and 2:00 P.M.). Obviously, this arrangement adds two hours a week (plus getting-there-and-back time) to your already overworked life. If that is more than you can afford, consider the thriftier arrangement of holding small groups only every other week. Or, more thriftily yet, on discussion days divide the class into four mini-classes: fifteen students meet from 11:00 to 11:30, fifteen from 11:30 to noon, and the remaining two groups meet earlier or later. Although students will have less face-to-face time, they will learn more.

As an alternative version, you can divide the class into two mini-classes (thirty at 11:00, thirty at 11:30), and then divide each of them into half again. In other words, two break-out groups will be discussing simultaneously for thirty minutes while you commute between them.

Before Each Discussion Begins

A week or so in advance of each small-group meeting, I recommend that you distribute a memo to accompany the assigned

Figure 6.1. How to Help a Discussion Succeed

INVITATION
Why do I care about this reading assignment and why do I believe you will care?

READING QUESTIONS
What should you keep your eye (and highlighter pen) focused on?

1.

2.

3.

DISCUSSION QUESTIONS

What are the main issues and implications?
(In one or two paragraphs, please write your responses to the following:)

1.

2.

---

reading (see Figure 6.1). Ideally, this handout will consist of three parts: an invitation; reading questions; and discussion questions.

Invitation: Why do I care about this reading assignment and why do I believe you will care? This may seem merely like clearing your throat before getting to the main point. Then again, let me remind you about the different states of mind with which you and your students approach the book or article. You have read it already. You're familiar with its intellectual context (which school of thought it belongs to, which side of a controversy it exemplifies). For your students, the assignment is like a blind date. They haven't heard of the author or read the material. All they know is that for some reason—a good one, they hope—you have told them to spend a few hours with the book or article. If you tell them why you and other scholars care about it, you will not only increase their motivation, but also focus their minds.

Here's one example:

Anne Moody's *Coming of Age in Mississippi* is a southern story, a black story, and a woman's story. Most of all, it's a powerful and exciting story by someone who was almost your age when she wrote it. Moody was born in 1940, and wrote this memoir in the mid-1960s at the height of the civil rights movement. It provides compelling testimony about this turning point in our history.

Here's a more specific handout from a syllabus on the "Anthropology of Globalization."

Kathryn Dudley's *The End of the Line* gives a detailed account of the aftermath of Chrysler Corporation's shutdown of auto assembly plants in Kenosha, Wisconsin, in 1988. Over 5,000 people lost their jobs, and the larger economic effects profoundly changed Kenosha. Since the 1930s the community had literally built itself around the auto industry as auto industry representatives lured people to Kenosha with the promise of continuing industrial progress and economic prosperity. Kenosha's transformation and the social drama that revolved around industrial decline and economic change offer us a rich example of many of the processes that we have studied in Anthropology 50, such as: deindustrialization; the trend toward a service economy; outsourcing; downsizing; and offshoring. The most important contribution that this ethnography makes to this class is its demonstration of relationships between larger global processes and local communities as it puts human faces and voices to the sometimes abstract notions of globalization.[11]

Reading Questions: What should you keep your eye (and highlighter pen) focused on? Once you've oriented your students and aroused their interest, pose several questions to accompany them through the text. These questions will guide your students as they read, help them see what's important (that is, what you're looking for), and define what they should understand when they reach the last page. The preceding anthropology handout, for example, asks, "How were people and groups affected differently by the Chrysler plant closing, depending on their occupation, class, gender, or place in the community?"

At this point you may be reacting as many professors have (including myself during my early years of teaching): "Why should I spoon-feed my students?" In response, I would point out that there's a difference between preparing the students to engage in learning and doing the learning for them. Put yourself in their mental shoes. Think back, for example, to that music appreciation class when you were supposed to analyze a Bartok string quartet, or to the archaeology class where the professor set two colorless, shapeless objects on the table and asked, "What meanings do you draw?" Do you remember that awful sense of paralysis? A few stepping-stone questions given beforehand help students begin grappling with the challenge. And you will be teaching them how to read a text in your field.

For instance, consider the reading questions for *Coming of Age in Mississippi*:

1. What do you think were the four or five turning points in her life? (We'll use these to "outline" the book.) Insert bookmarks so that you can easily locate your turning points.
2. How does she portray blacks? And whites? What did others in her family think about race? (As you read, keep track of specific examples.)
3. What part does Martin Luther King Jr. play in this history?

Discussion Questions: What are the main issues and implications? Whereas Reading Questions point toward the text, Discussion Questions point toward the classroom. They preview the open-ended, controversial issues that you foresee emerging out of the reading. Or to say it in cognitive terms, Reading Questions are about understanding, and Discussion Questions are about thinking.

For *Coming of Age in Mississippi*, one might ask:

1. By the end of her memoir, how does Moody justify her position on civil rights? Do you agree?
2. If Moody were to visit our campus today, what would she say about race relations among students?

And, for *The End of the Line*, "What does this book tell us about the rhetorics and realities of globalization?"

You may be wondering, "If I spell out the issues, haven't I turned the discussion into a recitation?"

No, these questions have many possible answers; your students will take the discussion in various unpredictable directions.

"But if I 'show my cards' by announcing my questions ahead of time," you persist, "how will I lead students Socratically toward the insights I have in mind?"

Yes, you will be forfeiting surprise and thereby forfeiting some control. But by sharing the cognitive structure with the students, you will improve the discussion. The more prepared they are, the more successfully they will engage the interesting, higher levels of discussion. As a result, you will be relieved of having to master-mind the discussion's path step by step. Instead of conducting while writing the score of an orchestra, you're leading a jazz ensemble. In sum, it's not in your self-interest to withhold lower-level information (key themes, things to look out for) or to keep secret the significant issues.

You will improve discussion not only by distributing questions ahead of time, but also by asking students to *write their responses*. Instead of that initial awkward silence as they mobilize their ideas, students will be ready to speak. In particular, the shyer or more introspective ones will find it easier to participate because they can paraphrase or simply read the response they already hold in their hands.

Just as you need to define explicitly what kind of discussion you are staging (recitation, conversation, and/or seminar), you also must spell out how you will deal with these written responses. Are you going to collect them after class? If so, are you going to grade them? If so, by what criteria? Reward and punishment play a crucial part—an ominous part—in the teaching/learning relationship.

Consider how one history professor defines this assignment in her syllabus:

You must write short reaction papers for six of the eight discussion sections. What is a "reaction paper"? It is a paper in which you react to what you have read for that day's discussion. You may react in any way you like—with horror, with glee, with detached reflection. In other words, you can write about whatever you like— as long as you react in some way to the reading assigned for the discussion section. You can compare what the source describes in a past time to circumstances in our own time. Or you can try to understand the activities described in the source in its historical context. Or you can offer an outraged analysis of the source. Or anything else. In other words, this assignment has no correct approaches and no right answers; it simply asks you to tussle with the reading on your own.

These reaction papers should be 250–400 words in length.

Needless to say, they should be careful, thoughtful, and well written, but we will read them with an awareness that they are "reaction papers" rather than polished essays. We intend to resist the urge to correct grammar and to worry overmuch about style, and we will focus instead on appreciating the content of your reaction.

Although these reaction papers are required, they are not graded.[12]

Many professors prefer to grade such writings, and students in turn want their effort rewarded. In that case, I recommend a minimal grading system because it is less likely to induce students to give safe answers (that is, "what the teacher is looking for"). For example, "Grades will usually be ✓ (adequate); sometimes + (outstanding); occasionally − (we need to confer)."

ELECTRONIC DISCUSSION

Instead of hard-copy handouts from you and hand-ins from students, you can conduct some of this process online. To lay the groundwork for each in-class discussion, you may save some labor (and paper) by distributing your study questions via e-mail. But that's merely efficiency, not pedagogy. You can employ the new technology more creatively if, a day before in-class discussion, you assign a student to pose questions about the reading assignment in an electronic forum such as Blackboard. In effect, this student serves as the teaching assistant. Or go a step further. Assign a student to write a brief critique of the reading assignment and a second student to write a rebuttal. Or take one additional step and invite (or require) their classmates to add their comments, creating an academic chat room. In any case, all members of the course are required to have read these commentaries before classtime.

According to professors who have added this electronic dimension to their repertoire, it has invigorated discussions in class. Students develop a personal investment in the topic. Shy students become more involved because they find it easier to write than speak to a group.

But these gains don't come without a price on your part and your students' as well. Are you creating substantive assignments? Are all students reading them faithfully and punctually? Are they writing thoughtful comments? Are you monitoring their responses? And most important, are you integrating the electronic forum continuously into the weekly work of the course? Unless you and they devote steady energy and attention, you risk the "empty restaurant syndrome," which deters potential participants.[13]

TROUBLESHOOTING

Despite your best efforts, a discussion section may begin to falter or, worse, bog down completely. You'll notice one or more dysfunctional symptoms. Before class, students are reading newspapers or staring stolidly ahead rather than chatting and smiling. During class, seemingly interminable silences (twenty to thirty seconds) elapse between one comment and the next. Only a few students are participating; the rest avoid your eyes. In mounting desperation you begin calling on students, which only increases the passive resistance.

After two such meetings, you walk toward the next one with a sour taste in your mouth, wishing you didn't have to attend. The students greet you with silence. The discussion moves even more gelatinously than usual. Finally you ask, in an accusing or plaintive tone, "How many of you have done the reading?" Most students raise their hands. "Why aren't you talking, then?" you say.

"Well, the book was kind of, like, dry," Jim says.

"And weird," someone calls out.

"I liked it," Evelyn says, "but I didn't understand what you're looking for?"

The rest, as usual, say nothing.

Clearly the teaching/learning relationship among your students and yourself is faltering. At this point you don't need to try harder. You need to try something altogether different.

But before you do anything, you must first diagnose why the group process has stalled. It makes no sense to fix the carburetor if you need a new battery. The possible culprits range across the pedagogical continuum:

- a cognitive problem: for example, reading assignments are more suitable to graduate students than undergraduates; and/or you haven't issued study questions to guide them through the reading;
- an interpersonal problem: for example, two particularly vocal students are intimidating; or you're intimidating because you (challenge, tease, frown, use Latin phrases, etc.);
- a logistical problem: for example, the chairs are bolted in rows and inhibit discussion; or the section meets at 1:00 P.M., when students are drowsily digesting lunch;
- an attitude problem on your part: how curious are you about their thinking and learning and about them as persons?;
- some combination of the above.

As a first step, ask your students to write down their answers—anonymously, of course—to some diagnostic questions. You can simply hand out blank index cards and ask, "What is going well? What needs to be improved or changed?" (In keeping with the principle that teaching is relational, you may also write your own response.) You can now take the cards home, ponder what you learn from them, and report your conclusions to the class next time. Or you may prefer to collect the cards, shuffle them, deal them out. At this point you have two choices. Either everyone reads a card aloud, and you facilitate a discussion of "what's wrong and how should we fix it?" Or, because learning is relational and therefore you may be part of the problem, ask a student to take charge while you leave the room. Explain that you will return in ten to fifteen minutes to hear their report.

Instead of this open-ended diagnostic, you can devise more focused questions. For example:

- Compared to other courses you've taken, is the reading more difficult, less difficult, or about the same?
- To what extent have you participated in discussion? Why not more?

Or even more specifically, distribute a "critical incident questionnaire":

- At what moment in class this week were you most engaged?
- At what moment were you most distanced?
- What action by anyone in the room this week did you find most affirming or helpful?
- What action did you find most confusing or intimidating?
- What surprised you most about the class this week?[14]

Either go through the shuffle-and-read-aloud procedure, or collect the replies, ponder them, discuss them with a colleague if you're feeling perplexed or defensive, and develop a strategy to resuscitate the discussion.

As yet another strategy, create groups, ask them to evaluate the discussions, and then have them appoint delegates to report to you what the groups said.

This chapter is the longest so far. That surprised me until I realized that discussion is a far more complex pedagogical activity than lecturing. Begin with the teacher's purposes, multiply (or divide) them by the presence of fifteen or twenty individuals, factor in everything from time of day to classroom architecture, and you're contending with awesome calculations.

Awesome but probably familiar. If you were a teaching assistant, you have already begun to master this mode of teaching. I hope that these suggestions add to your repertoire and success.

On the other hand, you likely haven't experimented with student activities other than discussion. If you're ready to learn about these, please turn to the next chapter.

7 / Broadening the Learning Environment

So far we have focused on four kinds of pedagogical activities: *listen, read, talk,* and *write.* These ingredients constitute the usual recipes for teaching and learning. Now let's expand your repertoire even further. This chapter will sketch more adventurous ways in which your students can learn by working collaboratively and, in some cases, producing more than words on paper or in air. A list of verbs will give a hint of what's to come: debate, elect, simulate, interview, perform, construct, exhibit.

Some of these activities can be initiated with minimal preparation and completed in as few as ten minutes. Others require more elaborate planning, by you as well as your students, and take place over several class periods. Knowing how busy you are, I'm not suggesting that you cook up all or even half of them. I do hope, though, that you try one or two. You'll discover that—like a teaspoon of rum in a pound cake—they energize the classroom in exciting ways. Work takes on a playful quality. Students experiment and explore. They become motivated not primarily by you the teacher, but by the project itself.

OPEN-ENDED WRITING

Instead of asking students to show how much they have learned of what you taught, design open-ended writing assignments. A psychology instructor, for example, might ask them to write a poem from the perspective of a schizophrenic. In a religious studies course, you can invite them to create a dialogue between a theist and an atheist.[1]

PANEL DISCUSSION

Classrooms typically include a single voice of authority. With minimal preparation, you can introduce other perspectives by staging a panel discussion. Ask a few student volunteers, or invite two colleagues, to discuss a topic. You not only will add refreshingly new voices, but you will enable students to recognize that "truth" is complex and contested.

DEBATES AND ROLE-PLAYING

To multiply students' voices and roles, consider the following three formats.

(1) Stage a debate between political candidates (Lincoln versus Douglas) or ideological spokespersons (Darwin versus the Archbishop of Canterbury; "pro-life" versus "pro-choice"; environmentalist versus logging company versus government regulators). Ask for volunteers who will lead the debate. Assign pertinent reading. After the debaters speak, the audience poses questions and, in the end, casts a vote.

(2) Instead of only a few debaters, you can enlist *all* students, even in a large class. In your homework assignment, tell them to come prepared to defend either side of the issue. After they've taken their seats, divide them randomly, perhaps along the middle aisle so that the "pro" students can turn to face the "con" students. You serve as moderator. At the end, you may choose to ask students to vote for the position they find more convincing.

Artificial though this exercise may sound, it exerts surprising intellectual impact. In a class on the American Revolution, for example, students divided into two groups, Prime Minister Grenville versus colonial spokesmen, and argued about why England should or should not levy the Stamp Tax. Afterward, many participants shook their heads, saying, "I never realized that the English had a defensible point of view."

How much of your precious class time will these two types of role-playing require? As much or as little as you choose. You may allocate one class for student teams to prepare and a second to debate and a third to debrief. Or (as with the Grenville example) you may compress the three phases into a single hour. Either way, your preparation time will be the same as for a regular discussion. Indeed, it may be less because you don't have to facilitate the back-and-forth among students.

(3) If you want students to work with more complex role-playing situations, consider the following options. A trial (of Joan of Arc, Galileo, Oscar Wilde, or Osama bin Laden, for example), in which groups are assigned to serve as prosecutor, defense, witnesses, judge, and jury, is particularly engaging. As students prepare, reenact, and then debrief, they use the trial as a window on the social, political, religious, and economic forces in the society.

As an alternative format, you might stage a "meeting of the minds" panel. In a psychology course, for example, Sigmund Freud, B. F. Skinner, and Carl Rogers would discuss the causes of teenage pregnancy.[2] In a political theory course, Immanuel Kant, Thomas Hobbes, and John Rawls would argue whether to grant women the right to vote.

You can also stage a constitutional convention, or a Parent Teacher Association meeting about school busing, or a hospital ethics committee discussing whether a comatose patient should be taken off life support. The possibilities are limited only by your field and your inventiveness. Keep in mind, though, that role-playing works best when it involves conflict or choice.

In order for students to perform their roles effectively and intelligently, they need to work with a lot of evidence beforehand. You can assemble it for them by distributing handouts or assigning websites. Or you can tell them to find it on their own (although you may choose to expedite the process by providing a list of sources).

You also need to spell out the procedures once they arrive in the classroom. It's a good idea to schedule the event in two or even three phases: one class when students in each role confer and formulate their ideas; a second class when they enact their roles; and possibly a third class when everyone steps out of their roles and discusses the meaning of what they have done.

More specifically, you need to define the rules of play. How will different groups interact (verbally? in writing?); with what currency (ideas? votes? "money"?); and with what goal (does someone "win"? if so, how is that determined?).

In this chapter's appendixes (Appendixes 7.1–7.3), you will find the rules for three games: the ideological and political conflict on the eve of the American Civil War; postwar Reconstruction in the South; and the tension between scientific research, environmentalism, and corporate profits.

CASE STUDY

Many law schools and business schools structure their entire curriculum around the case-study method because it teaches students to apply abstract theory and analysis to the complexities of real-life situations. You can derive similar benefits if you devise a case for your undergraduate course.

Essentially a case is a story. Or, to frame it more academically, it's "a research study with a sample of one."[3] A case presents a thought-provoking issue, arouses empathy with its characters, and challenges students to decide "What would you do?" It can be a two-paragraph vignette taken from a newspaper or a lengthy document replete with statistical tables and memos, a video containing interviews, or a piece of fiction. Whatever the length and format, a case assembles information that students assess and then employ in working out a decision or solution. In other words, you're asking them to collaborate and learn from experience.[4]

In a political science course, the case may entail a foreign policy crisis (for example, the kidnapping of American missionaries in Pakistan), with students assigned to different interest groups advising the president. In a public policy course, students might have to balance the medical and environmental benefits of an antismoking ordinance against the costs to business and the infringement on personal rights. (For a sample case, see Appendix 7.4. For dozens of excellent cases in various disciplines, consult the websites listed in the endnote.)[5]

Cases such as these require considerable homework on your part in order to recreate the situation in all its complexity. But you can also foster the same kind of learning with less extensive materials. Here's an excerpt from a case about communication and gender roles:

Study questions for students:
1. Identify examples of "mind reading" and describe the impact on Martha and Andy's discussion.
2. Identify communication that fosters a defensive interpersonal climate.
3. Do you perceive any relationship-level meanings that aren't being addressed in this conversation?
4. How do male and female role-expectations affect the relationship and the communication between Martha and Andy?

The text:
Andy and Martha married five years ago when both completed graduate school. Last week Andy got the job offer of his dreams, with one problem: He would have to move 1,500 miles away. Martha loves her current job and has no interest in moving or in living apart. Andy sees this job as one that can really advance his career. For the past week they have talked and argued continuously about the job offer. Tonight, while they are preparing dinner in their kitchen, they have returned to the topic once again. We join them midway in their discussion, just as it is heating up.

ANDY: So today I was checking on the costs for flights from here to Seattle. If we plan ahead for visits, we can get round-trip flights for around $300. That's not too bad.

MARTHA: While you're thinking about finances, you might consider the cost of renting a second apartment out there. We agreed last night that it would be too expensive to live apart.

ANDY: I never agreed to that. Martha, can't you understand how important this job is to my career?

MARTHA: And what about our marriage? I suppose that's not important?

ANDY: (He grabs a knife and begins cutting an onion.) I never said that! If you'd pull with me on this one, our marriage would be fine. You're just not . . . .

MARTHA: (She slams a pot on the stove.) Not what? Not willing to be the traditional supportive wife, I assume.

ANDY: (He grimaces, puts down the knife, and turns to face Martha.) That isn't what I was going to say. I never asked you to be a traditional wife or to be anything other than who you are, but I want you to let me be myself, too.

MARTHA: If you want to be yourself, then why did you get married? Marriage is about more than just yourself—it's about both of us and what's good for the two of us. You're not thinking of us at all.[6]

Whatever the subject matter, a case typically involves a dilemma that requires students to apply concepts from the course as they weigh alternative decisions. In preparing one, you need to assemble the data they will work with. More basically, you need to be clear about which concepts are at stake—that is, about your pedagogical purpose. As Wilbert McKeachie aptly says, "The teacher needs to think, 'What is this case a case of?' "[7]

INTERVIEW, POLL, FOCUS GROUP, OR SURVEY

Rather than working with other people's evidence, students can create their own. In an urban sociology course, they may observe, interview, and/or photograph at a downtown street corner. History teachers have discovered the benefits of asking students to interview a parent or relative about some past experience—for example, service in the Vietnam War or the choice of a career/job—and to write an oral history. In a psychology course on gender roles, students can design, implement, and interpret an opinion poll, or they can organize focus groups.

Projects such as these produce an extraordinarily vibrant learning environment. For one thing, students practice the skills of a discipline. They are not only reading what sociologists, psychologists, et al. have written; they are *doing* sociology, psychology, etc. As a result, they are working with the zeal that accompanies personal discovery. Like "Outward Bound" participants, they are exploring uncharted territory and returning to show-and-tell what they found. In a word, they become teachers.

Indeed, many faculty have included students as collaborators in their own research projects. Both teaching and research have in common, after all, the process of learning. Thomas Goodwin, professor of chemistry at Hendrix College in Arkansas, studies the biochemistry of elephants. His students work alongside him at a nearby sanctuary, trying to identify the chemical compounds that may reveal how animals communicate.[8]

PUBLIC EXHIBIT

You can expand the learning environment even further by redefining the audience. Instead of having students present their work to you and one another, invite them to present it to the public beyond the classroom. In so doing, you add authenticity to what often seems to be an artificial process. You move from "the ivory tower" to "the real world." Jacquelyn Hall's students at the University of North Carolina created an exhibit at the local museum about Chapel Hill's school desegregation in the 1960s, combining interviews, archival research, and photographs. Chad Richardson, a sociologist in Texas, not only sent his students out to do ethnographic interviews in the Lower Rio Grande Valley. He also created an archive of their findings and helped some of them publish their stories.[9] On a less elaborate scale, you can schedule an afternoon conference when your students talk about their term papers to friends, parents, and the public at large. Or they can be curators for an exhibit of paintings in an art gallery.

Let your students brainstorm. Their ingenuity may take your breath away. Halfway through a freshman seminar on "Coming of Age in the 1950s and 1960s," I urged my students to devise a collaborative final project. "Create a magazine, for example," I suggested, "or a photo-collage." "Boring," they replied. After a week of brainstorming, they came up with the idea of an exhibit of seven suitcases. They filled each suitcase with clothing, books, writings, music, and other evidence to represent a different type of youth from those decades: a middle-class college student, a Beat, a civil rights worker, a hippie, and so on. "What should we title the exhibit?" I asked. A student smiled and said, "All Packed and Ready to Grow." During the one-day showing, faculty, friends, parents, and total strangers peered into the suitcases, munched refreshments, and congratulated the students on their accomplishment.

The more room you leave for students to define the direction and outcome, the more they may delight you with how much and how creatively they learn. On the other hand, because they are unused to autonomy, they may falter, bicker, stray into blind alleys, or settle for triviality. Some students may abdicate responsibility, leaving their classmates to do the lion's share of the work. Some may be shy and others domineering.

You will likely need to serve as a facilitator, helping the group to define their goals, procedures, and schedule—their social contract. How will they apportion tasks, set deadlines, monitor progress, express complaints, and settle disagreements? The group will also need to be clear as to how you, or they, or you and they together will grade their work.

Even after spelling out their social contract, however, small groups may end up falling short of the goals that you and they had hoped for. That's the risk in all formats of pedagogy, of course, whether a teacher-dominated lecture or a freewheeling discussion. No type of teaching/learning comes with a guarantee of success. In more open-ended formats, however, you are facilitator more than teacher, so you are exerting less control and certainly have less sense of control. Your students are working out the shape of their projects on their own. Instead of their asking "what do you have in mind?" you're asking them "how is it going?" Together, you're playing by unfamiliar rules, or more likely inventing them as you go, which will be alternately disquieting and exhilarating.

As you have heard throughout this book, I am not dictating the right or best way to teach. Only you can decide whether or when to try some of the pedagogical recipes in this chapter. But just as you encourage your students to venture beyond their familiar mental boundaries—because that is what learning means—I encourage you to do the same with your teaching.

Appendix 7.1: A Civil War/Peace Game

The time: November 7, 1860.

The situation: Lincoln (Rep., Ill.) was elected president of the United States yesterday, but he will take office only on March 4, 1861. In the meantime, Buchanan (Dem., Pa.) will continue as "lame duck" president.

The threat of secession by southern states looms on the horizon. Today the South Carolina legislature is discussing whether or not to call for a state convention that, in turn, would vote to secede from the Union.

The question: In 1859 Senator William H. Seward (Rep., N.Y.) spoke of an "irrepressible conflict" between North and South. Is it irrepressible? Your task is to find a compromise to avoid war. The key will be to get *at least three* groups to agree on that compromise.

The players: The class is divided into five groups.

1. Abolitionists: In objecting not simply to the extension of slavery, but to any action that implicitly accepts slavery, many of you have favored dissolving the Union. Many of you also have been pacifists. Are you going to change your stand now that Lincoln will soon take office, and southern secession seems imminent? What influence can you exert, during this crisis, to bring abolition closer? Which deals can you strike with other groups?

2. Republicans: You are a collection of experienced state leaders who have heard threats of secession before. You believe secession to be illegal and also economically absurd. Can you preserve the Union without war? What kind of political or economic deal can you work out with the Unionists or the Fire-eaters to stay in the Union? Can you think of persuasive arguments to make to them?

3. Northern Democrats: You endorse slavery where it exists and will let it expand according to the policy of "popular sovereignty."

4. Southern Democrats: You are a collection of experienced former Whig leaders who have been dismayed by the steadily growing friction between North and South. You accept slavery as necessary, but you are less dogmatic than the Fire-eaters on the questions of extending slavery and the Fugitive Slave Law. Can you offer compromises (political and/or economic) on these or other issues without losing political support within your states?

5. Southern "Fire-eaters": You have been demanding that the North accept both the Fugitive Slave Law and the extension of slavery into unorganized territories. Are there any concessions you would make to preserve the Union? What is the price (political, economic, military?) you would ask to stay in the Union?

The Press will be played by the instructor.

The procedure: Groups will be allowed to communicate with each other only in writing. If you want to issue a press release, write PRESS on the carbon and give it to the instructor.

In order to perform well, you must come to class with a clear understanding of the general situation in 1860 and of what your group wants. Therefore, you must have read the assigned readings.

Planning day is Monday. Playing day is Wednesday.[10]

Appendix 7.2: Reconstructing the Union, 1866: A Game in Constitutional Amending

The situation: Spring 1866, the Joint Committee on Reconstruction. After President Johnson's plan for reconstruction apparently failed, both houses of Congress organized the Joint Committee last December to devise an alternative plan of reconstruction. The committee's plan is to take the form of a constitutional amendment in order to secure the plan's enactment. How do you propose to reunite the Union, and what do you propose to do about the four million freed slaves? Numerous hearings will be held to gain various viewpoints.

The task: Draft a constitutional amendment to be presented on the floor of the House of Representatives and Senate.

The players:

1. Radical Republicans: A minority on the committee, you have long supported abolition and want to punish severely the South for its rebellion. You want to see the southern ruling class overthrown by imposing a northern-style free-labor economy; the disfranchisement of Confederates and confiscation of their lands; and for freedmen the provision of suffrage and confiscated land. You fear that representation of blacks will give southern states too much power and perhaps enable them to conquer Washington in peace after failing in war. How can you achieve your goals?

2. Moderate Republicans: Dominating the Joint Committee, you generally want to ensure the repudiation of secession and the confirmation of emancipation, while preventing former rebels from regaining control over the South. Most of you believe that Johnson did not go far enough in ensuring northern victory. Although you fear the resurgence of the Democratic Party, you share its antipathy toward black suffrage. Confident that you are the majority bloc in Congress, which provisions do you advocate, and how can you garner additional support from either side?

3. Conservative Republicans: Comprising about 20 percent of Congress, you are basically content with Johnson's program, though some of you would like to see greater protection for blacks. You have tended to support the party vote. You will sway the ultimate vote. Will you now stand more rigidly on what you believe?

4. Democratic lobbyists: You are eager to allow the South to reconstruct itself and determine its own terms of loyalty and election of representatives. Most of you have opposed emancipation from its inception and even called for the end of the war as a result. You fear the attempts of Radical

Republicans to make Reconstruction a revolution and have admired Johnson's continued attempts to resist such corruption and to sustain states' rights. Although you comprise but one quarter of the House of Representatives, you sense increasing support from Johnson. Can you persuade some of the more conservative and moderate Republicans to vote against radical proposals and convince them that the nation is against them?

5. Woman/black suffrage testifiers: You are a group of suffragists, Freedmen's Bureau agents, and freedpeople who are seeking to gain support among the representatives for your policies. After living in the South, you have concluded that black suffrage is necessary to ensure black freedom. You see that the opportunity for a constitutional amendment has occurred only because of the turmoil of war and may not arise again for decades. Accordingly, you want to ensure not only black freedom, but also the freedom of women. How can you persuade congressmen of the need and justifiability for introducing black and female suffrage?

The procedure: The goal is consensus. The broader the congressional support, the more likely the public will support ratification. Remember that blacks comprise over 10 percent of the population and women over 50 percent. Members of each group will bring a written proposal of at least one aspect of a constitutional amendment, with a rationale for why such a provision is necessary. When the discussion opens, groups will meet individually and may either communicate in writing or by sending an emissary to meet with another group. Groups wishing to present a message to all groups and reveal information to the general public may give it to the instructor with "Press Release" written at the top.[11]

Appendix 7.3: Basic versus Applied Research Game

The time: The present.

The situation: There is a major controversy taking place these days in the scientific community regarding the value of various types of scientific research.

Meanwhile, the president has announced a new scientific research program. He says it will:

- help laid-off automobile workers;
- make U.S. products more competitive to sell in Eastern Europe;
- correct the United States–Japan trade imbalance by selling new goods and services to Japan.

The players:

1. Presidents of corporations (AT&T, Bell Labs, Ford, etc.)
2. Scientists doing basic research (the Human Genome Project; the Jet Propulsion Lab's Galileo Project)
3. Scientists doing applied research (Genentech)
4. Government employees (National Science Foundation; National Institutes of Health)
5. Environmental groups
6. Health-care professionals (Centers for Disease Control)

The questions:

- Which type of research should be pursued: basic, applied, or both?
- Who should support it?
- What percentage of funds and time should be allotted for each type?
- Based on your recommendations, what will happen in the future?
- What will happen if your recommendations are turned down?

Food for thought:

- Some basic scientific research has no foreseeable practical value other than "knowledge for knowledge's sake."
- Many technological, medical, and scientific breakthroughs were made possible only due to the knowledge gained by prior basic research.

Discussion questions:

- Can our nation afford to spend millions of dollars on research that may have no practical benefit?
- Should educational institutions concentrate on basic research, or should they be allowed to concentrate on research programs that might be more profitable in the end?

- Should Congress be allowed to tell the National Science Foundation and other research-funding organizations what types of scientific research should be supported?
- Does industry bear a responsibility to support basic research, since its technological and medical advances are often the result of someone else's basic work?[12]

Appendix 7.4: A Case of Mistaken Identity? The Psychology of Eyewitness Memory

In the past few months there has been a series of attacks on white and Asian women in a local neighborhood, and the police have been under pressure to solve the cases. You are the defense attorney representing Tyrone Briggs, who has been charged with aggravated assault in the crimes.

Tyrone is a nineteen-year-old high school basketball star who, at the time of the crimes, was living at 412 Jervay Place, the local housing project. Tyrone is 6′1″ tall, has long hair processed in Jeri curls, a broad flat nose, a large mole on his lip, and a severe stutter. The general description given by the witnesses (most of whom were the victims of the assaults) at the time of the attacks was that the attacker was in his early twenties, light-skinned, between 170 and 200 pounds, with a short afro and possibly a receding hairline. None of the victims mentioned a mole or a stutter at the time of the attacks.

You have recently read a defense attorney newsletter that outlines some of the problems with eyewitness identification and have looked at the National Institute of Justice's guidelines for law enforcement commissioned by the U.S. attorney general.[13] Based on your reading, you believe that Tyrone may be a victim of mistaken identification. However, the five victims and an African American man who briefly held the assailant at gunpoint have all identified Tyrone as the man who committed the crimes. You need to decide whether to hire an expert in eyewitness memory to testify at the trial. Because it costs money to hire the expert, you want to be reasonably certain that the expert witness will indeed cast doubt on the veracity of the victims' testimony.

The first witness was a Seattle University pre-med student who was taking a run around the campus track during the afternoon when she was attacked. As she was running, she noticed a man standing near the public restrooms. As she neared him, he called out to her, saying he had a question. As she got closer to him, he suddenly lunged at her with a serrated knife and began dragging her toward the restroom. She wriggled out of her sweatshirt and ran across the field toward the campus buildings while he yelled after her, "I'm going to get you!"

The second witness, an attorney, was attacked at 8:00 A.M. as she was walking toward the courthouse. A man jumped out of "nowhere," knocked her to the ground, and said repeatedly, "Give me your money. I'm going to stab you." He held a serrated knife in his hand. She fought back and he ran off, taking her purse and gym bag with him.

The third witness, a social worker, was attacked when she parked near the housing project on her way to the hospital. A man came around the corner and, walking quickly, pulled out a small steak knife and said, "Your purse or your money." She started screaming and the man ran away. The encounter lasted about half a minute and was the shortest attack.

The fourth witness, another social worker, was walking to work at the hospital when a man jumped out of the bushes and grabbed her. In a low conversational tone of voice he said, "I'm going to stab you in the head. Give me your money." She offered him the five dollars that she had. He said it was not enough and began putting his hand up her skirt. She started screaming, kicking, and scratching, and managed to get away. He ran off in the opposite direction.

The fifth witness, an X-ray technician, was walking to work at the hospital when she saw a man standing in the darkened entrance to an alleyway. She kept walking. Seconds later she was laying on the ground, dazed. The assailant had hit her in the back of the head with a fence post. He then proceeded to punch her several times in the face and dragged her into a vacant apartment in Jervay Place, where he tore off her clothes and attempted to rape her. Another man, Karl Vance, opened the door to the vacant apartment, shouting, "Hold it. I have a gun!" Mr. Vance then yelled to his girlfriend, who lived at 410 Jervay Place, to call the cops. The attacker bolted through the back door.

Within two months of the first attack and a month after the last attack the police had arrested Tyrone. The same day Tyrone was arrested, Karl Vance picked Tyrone's picture out of a series of twenty-one photos and indicated that he was absolutely positive of his identification. The next day the police obtained a search warrant and searched Tyrone's home. They were unable to find any stolen property, knives, or distinctive clothing. Later that day, the police brought four of the victims down to the precinct to view a lineup. The police informed the women that it was to be expected that they might have an emotional response to seeing their attacker again; however, the women were assured that the attacker could not see them.

After an hour, the police informed the women that they could not get enough people together to ensure that the person in custody would have a fair lineup so they would have to do a photo lineup instead. Because Tyrone had a prominent mole on his lip, the police followed standard procedure and made sure that all of the photos had a similar mole so that Tyrone would not stand out. All four of the victims looked at the photo lineup and selected Tyrone's picture. However, they indicated that they were uncertain and chose the person who looked most like their attacker. The fifth victim selected Tyrone from the same photo lineup a week later.

One week later the victims were brought back in for a live lineup. Tyrone was in the line up with six other African American men who looked similar to him. The officer who conducted the lineup did not conceal Tyrone's mole or ensure that everyone had a similar feature. The officer who conducted the lineup had members of the lineup repeat phrases that were said at the time of the crimes. One of the victims noted in her written statement that the man in the lineup stuttered and her attacker did not. Several others noted that he seemed "nervous" because of the stutter. However, all of the victims as well as Karl Vance selected Tyrone.

As the defense lawyer, you need to decide whether to hire the expert witness. Questions for you to ponder include:

- Do you think that Tyrone Briggs might be a victim of false identification? Why or why not?
- What factors are present that make the witnesses reliable?
- What factors are present that make the witnesses unreliable?[14]

8 / Evaluating and Grading

Two students are chatting at the end of the semester.

"What did you get out of Dominguez's course?"

"I got a C-plus."

"Tough luck. I got a B."

Of course one shouldn't hear them literally. They "got" more than an alphabet letter out of all those lectures, discussions, writing assignments, and other activities on which Professor Dominguez lavished so much effort. Still, this all-too-familiar student conversation carries a useful warning. Grades claim disproportionate attention. They are scores required by the dean, Phi Beta Kappa, graduate admissions committees, and other governing powers beyond your classroom. They compete with, and sometimes overshadow, the process of learning that is their raison d'être. This holds true not only for students but also for faculty. After a teacher has been reading sixty scribbled essays about "why the Ancient Mariner killed the albatross," vacillating between a "B-minus" and "C-plus" for this answer, a "B" or "B-plus" for that one, he/she not only becomes exhausted. He/she also has to resist becoming a judge whose sentences reward or punish rather than teach. This state of mind does not befit a learning environment. Imagine a yoga class or a pottery workshop in which students receive a "B" or "C."

This chapter will deal with grading on a practical level, offering various methods for you to save time and also to be fair. But first things first. Pedagogy before practicality. Because we want a student to "get" more than a grade out of your course, let's begin by discussing evaluation.

To evaluate is to take stock. It's an occasion for helping students understand how much progress they have made. It continues your half of the teacher-student dialogue. In other words, how far have they gone with those promises you announced in your syllabus?

Teachers typically discover the answer by "examining" students' knowledge. A good exam question serves as a good teaching tool; a bad or mediocre one impedes learning. Framing effective questions is a tricky skill to which scholars have devoted entire chapters or books. Rather than resorting to mere tidbits of what they say, let me direct you toward their own writings.[1] Let's focus here on the ways you may respond to your students' blue books or essays.

Just as you want your students to learn by writing, you also want them to learn from your comments on their writing. So you need to schedule several exams, quizzes, or other writing opportunities at intervals during the semester. Then these exams or "tests" will also instruct.[2] An exam is the continuation of teaching by other means.

Here we return to the difference between *knowing* and *understanding*. When your student finds a "D" penciled at the top of his or her essay, that student knows that he/she has fallen dismally short of the goal but doesn't necessarily understand why. Your evaluative comments begin to build the bridge toward understanding by spelling out the reasons that lurk behind that "D." "The essay lacks a thesis paragraph," you may write. "Also, it doesn't complete the comparison with Chinese child-rearing and fails to cite evidence from Terrell's article." (Needless to say, I assume you will phrase your critiques more humanely. When faced with entirely negative or hostile evaluations, people react defensively and/or give up. That is, your comments become counterproductive. Appendix 8.1 to this chapter provides guidelines for how to write productive comments.)

Your comments are only half a bridge, however, because evaluation expresses only your side of the educational dialogue. Until your student demonstrates that he/she understands how to write a thesis paragraph and until he/she cites Terrell's article, you can't be sure how much he/she has learned from your comments. So you would do well to conclude your critique with: "Let's talk about this. Can you come to my office hours on Tuesday?" or "Please rewrite page 3." This means extra work for you, as well as for the student, and we imagine both of you uttering a weary sigh. But preventive action now will pay off with a better essay next time.

When we turn to the opposite end of the spectrum, where a student finds an "A-minus" adorning his essay, the mood is happier, but your responsibility to evaluate remains the same. This student knows that he/she has succeeded, but you need to explain why that grade was warranted. After all, the student may attribute the success to the accuracy of the facts; or think that you're rewarding him/her for mimicking your point of view; or believe that he/she somehow "got lucky." You will give the student intellectual perspective—an understanding that applies beyond this one essay—by identifying the accomplishments. "I particularly like how your argument doesn't simplify the issue to black and white. For example, you don't romanticize Samoan childhood. Another strength: the transition sentences work well to tie the essay together from one paragraph to the next." Comments such as these go beyond "feel-good" applause. They analyze the components of successful learning and thereby hand the student the tools for building more such essays.

EVALUATING TEACHING AND LEARNING

Because teaching entails a two-way process, your students' success or failure is also, to some extent, yours. The extent varies, of course. If a student doesn't care or doesn't try, the responsibility is his or hers. Suppose, on the other hand, that more than half of your class receive a "D" on the first midterm because they have misunderstood "romanticism." Does this signal a problem on their part or yours, or some of both? Or is some other factor at fault (for example, the textbook or the wording of the question)? To figure out what has gone wrong, you undertake a detective hunt. You examine the question (two paragraphs that now seem more convoluted than precise), reread your lecture notes (a nuanced—too nuanced?—contrast between "romantic" and "individualistic"), scrutinize the textbook (a single opaque paragraph), and interview a few students (each understood the question differently).

This is the kind of evaluation I hope you won't be doing—retrospective and rueful, in the wake of a breakdown in student-teacher communication. You will likely avoid it if you institute a variety of intermediate evaluations, taking stock not at the end or even at midterm but at numerous moments en route. Here are four possibilities. At the same time as each of these interventions measures ("tests") what students have learned, they will give you feedback as to how effectively you have been teaching.

(1) Consider using an *in-class, short-answer quiz*. Teachers typically employ this as a policing tactic—coercing students to do the homework and grading how well they've done it. You can transform it into more of an evaluative device, however, if you make one or two alterations.

You can decide to give no grade. Mark wrong answers, so that students realize what they haven't understood. Require them to correct these answers with brief explanations of why they were incorrect. The only "grade" will be 100 percent. Indeed, you can take one step further away from grades and toward learning: instead of marking the quizzes yourself, ask students to do so. As soon as they finish writing, discuss each question. Students who wrote wrong answers will correct them or ask for help in understanding why they're wrong.

Even if you don't want to abandon grades, you will help your own cause by fashioning quizzes that go beyond recall and ask for understanding and thinking. Instead of multiple-choice or identification questions (which require lower-level skills, hence surface learning), you might use a format that focuses on drawing relationships and recognizing significance (and thus, higher-level skills and deeper learning). For one model, employed in a global history course, see Figure 8.1.

Figure 8.1. Drawing Relationships Quiz

The following five items are arranged as pairs. You have a twofold task. In no more than two sentences, (1) define each item in a pair and (2) draw a relationship between them that pertains to the context of our course.

Nonviolent resistance	Huey Newton
Cuban revolution	Che Guevara
Women's liberation	Miss America pageant
Cold War	Tet offensive
Decolonization	Franz Fanon

Sample Response:

Communism　　　　　　Japanese invasion of China

Mao Tse-tung led the Chinese Communist Party, espousing Marx's belief that a state-planned economy would result in equal distribution of wealth [brief definition]. When Japan invaded China as part of its World War II expansionism [brief definition], Mao became a popular nationalist leader because he resisted the foreign invasion [relationship].

Source: Alvis Dunn, Department of History, Guilford College, Greensboro, North Carolina.

(2) As a brief feedback device that is more open-ended, you can use the *sixty-second essay* (see chapter 5). The essay functions as a snapshot of how students have understood or misunderstood a single lecture, discussion, or reading assignment.

(3) More generally, devise a *graduated sequence* of exams or other writings. By waiting until mid-semester to assign a midterm, you keep students (and yourself) uncertain about their progress. Learning evolves in steps rather than in a single heroic bound. So begin early and modestly. For example, in the second week, distribute a short-answer quiz to measure how well students *comprehend* the key facts. In the third week, climb one rung of the cognitive ladder. Ask them to *interpret* those facts (evidence) in a mini-essay (250 words maximum) or mini-exam (fifteen min-

utes). "Using two pertinent examples, explain why . . . . In your first ('thesis') paragraph, state your argument." By providing such cramped space, you're signaling that quantity doesn't equal success. Students can't "regurgitate" everything they have read or memorized, so there's a better chance that they will focus on process.

In the fifth or sixth week, they'll be ready to undertake a full-length writing assignment.

(4) Ask students to *give feedback to one another*. After you've evaluated their first essays, select three along the spectrum from excellent to adequate, hand out (anonymous) copies, and ask students in small groups to rank them, using your criteria and articulating their reasons. A half hour later, bring students back together to compare their rankings and reasons with your own. Students often say these thirty-minute sessions were the most helpful of their college career in teaching them to write.

GRADING LEARNING

Curve or Straight?

You need to choose between grading on a curve or by a standard, and also between offering cumulative or noncumulative examinations. The decision is up to you, of course, but let me spell out the reasons for mine. Ken Bain's study of outstanding teachers found that the overwhelming majority graded on a standard and used cumulative major exams. They did so because they believed that grading on a curve pitted students against each other, which created a sense that examinations were a game to win rather than an opportunity to learn. In other words, the curve fostered strategic rather than deep learning. These professors wanted, instead, to help students achieve a standard in order to hold them to it. Likewise, they made exams cumulative to encourage students to grow. The bar was high, but students were given plenty of opportunities to try, to receive feedback, and to redouble their effort before earning a final judgment. According to Richard Light's interviews with thousands of Harvard students, these policies made them want to learn permanently rather than, as one of them put it, "kiss it all good-bye as soon as the examination was over."[3]

Whip or Carrot?

Grades matter. They sum up a student's achievement in a quantifiable form and determine academic success (dean's list, acceptance to law school) or failure (expulsion) or something in between. These scores, in turn, permit graduate schools and employers to rank applications. Grades matter as a kind of currency for getting ahead and therefore preoccupy the students who "get" them and the teachers who "give" them. "Getting and spending, we lay waste our powers," Wordsworth reminds us. Because grades matter, responsible teachers (power-holders) often feel obliged to spell out their policies in elaborate detail.

You may earn up to 100 points by completing the five assignments, two take-home essays, and three in-class examinations. Think of the first essay and the first exam as practice. They are shorter than the others and count for fewer points. Sixty points of 100 get you a D; 70 a C−; 88 a B+, etc. If necessary, I curve the grades to assure that at least 10 percent of the class receives an A or A−.[4]

At the same time, many teachers—especially teachers who are new to the responsibilities of power—spell out policies for delinquency.

A third of a grade will be subtracted for every six hours that a term paper is handed in beyond the deadline. Missed discussion sections will be excused and make-up exams offered only upon presentation of either an obituary about the deceased relative or a legal or medical document.

Regulations such as these deploy power to control students' behavior, but they also betray a fear of losing control. I empathize with this feeling because I remember all too well my own fears as I began teaching. "How will I make them do their work?" It's tempting to rely on the power of the grade as the solution, but I urge you to spurn the temptation. You may *de*grade the environment you're trying to foster. Grades exert surprisingly little effect on learning, and punitive policies tend to have negative effects.[5]

Let's start with the negative. The threat of low grades may prod some students to work harder. But it may just as likely cause others to manufacture excuses, cheat, become demoralized, or give up. "Pop" quizzes may enforce reading attendance but will also arouse resentment. Penalties for turning in papers late or for missing class may coerce compliance but don't teach a sense of responsibility. In other words, if you use grades as a pedagogical whip, you'll be reinforcing the working-to-get-a-grade mentality rather than a genuine learning environment.

Carrots work better than whips. Consider the following controlled experiment. One high school math teacher graded every homework assignment, counting the results as one-third of the students' final grade. A second teacher told students to spend half an hour every night on their homework, and to come to class with questions about problems they couldn't solve. This teacher gave only two grades—satisfactory or unsatisfactory—and invited students to revise their homework, which counted only 10 percent of the final grade. What were the effects of these policies? In the first class, some students who were scoring poorly stopped trying to succeed. Students in the second class, by contrast, kept handing in their homework because their mistakes were defined as a part of learning rather than a measure of personal worth.[6]

For better or worse, grades matter; the challenge is how to make them work for your purposes. Listen to how one professor (in his first course, I might add) couches his regulations within a pedagogical framework.

Late Papers: Numerous problems are lurking out there to help you miss assignment deadlines. Computer failures, family crises, and misreading the syllabus will all send you scrambling to complete papers on time. Plan ahead and be ready to work around computer problems. Papers are due at the beginning of the class period. Late papers will be docked a letter grade for every weekday they are overdue. (If a paper due on Thursday is turned in on the following Monday and earns an A, the grade will become a C.) If you know ahead of time that you will have a problem completing a paper on time, please contact me. By "ahead of time," I mean more than three days in advance of the deadline.

I am happy to discuss a paper or exam grade with you at any time. Talking to me about your graded assignments is a great way to learn how to improve throughout the semester. If you wish to have a grade reconsidered, you must first submit to me a written statement outlining your reasons, along with the paper or exam. This allows you to collect your thoughts and make your best case for a higher grade. In order for the assignment to remain fresh in both of our minds, you must submit this appeal within a week of receiving the grade.[7]

Some instructors have gone one step further, not counting off for lateness and focusing instead on students' responsibility to be on time. What do you think of the following policy for turning in short papers that students would share with one another?

If you do not submit a paper by the indicated date, there are several unavoidable and undesirable consequences. First, your colleagues will not benefit from your thinking, and you will not benefit from any feedback they can provide. Second, all papers are due on a Friday. I have reserved time in my own life in the following weekend to provide you with feedback. I will return your papers on the following Wednesday. If you submit your work late, I probably will not be able to look at it right away, and you may not get my feedback before the next paper is due. Your education will probably suffer, and it will just give you headaches you don't want to endure. If, for whatever reason, you cannot meet the deadline, please inform me and your colleagues by e-mail.[8]

Rubrics

A respectful, collaborative stance signals that you don't intend to play the adversarial student-teacher game. Still, it focuses only on

Figure 8.2. Criteria for a Successful Essay

1. Focus on the issue (does the writing deal with the problem?)
2. Evidence (does it support its position with adequate data?)
3. Coherence (does the argument hold together and move forward?)
4. Scope (does it deal with all important aspects of the problem?)
5. Originality

    A = excellent performance on all five criteria

    B = above average on four or excellent on some but flawed on others

    C = average across the board or above average in part but with significant flaws

    D = below average across the board

Source: Jeff Jones and Peter Filene, Department of History, University of North Carolina at Chapel Hill.

---

outcomes—the payoff—and therefore (ironically) honors the obsession with grades. To push grades into the background and learning into the foreground, you also need a collaborative policy for the early stage of the assignment—the input. How can you do that? The solution is remarkably simple: *spell out the criteria for success.*

In chapter 6 I encouraged you to "show your cards" to students before a discussion. That practice is even more advisable for writing assignments. When students ask, "What are you looking for? What do you have in mind?" don't be cagey or keep your expectations secret. Of course, you shouldn't give them the "right answers"; that would appropriate their half of the learning dialogue. But you should tell them how to go about developing their own answers. That's your half of the dialogue. Better to do it beforehand, laying the foundation for success, than afterward, trying to undo the damage.

You can provide this kind of advance notice by including in your syllabus a set of criteria—what is called a rubric. For example, see Figure 8.2 and the alternative versions in Appendixes 8.2 and 8.3.

In addition to a general rubric, you will also avoid misunderstanding and resentment in the teacher-student dialogue if you distribute a rubric for each writing assignment.

Before leaving this thorny topic of grading, let's address two possible apprehensions. First, disarming yourself of the grade-as-whip may make you feel vulnerable. Without this weapon, you wonder how you can coerce students to learn. But coercion is not the best incentive for learning. And coercion distracts you from teaching. Without the grade-as-whip, you will be relieved of playing police officer, double-checking alibis and doctors' notes while verifying signatures on attendance sheets.

Second, disarmament does not mean abandoning intellectual standards. On the contrary, instead of trying to control potential delinquents, you will be working with students to meet your best expectations. And given that offer—collaborative but also demanding—they are more likely to do their best.

SURVIVING

These strategies will improve your evaluating and grading. The more open and positive the ground rules, the more students succeed. The more they succeed, the less repair work you will have to do and the more you can fine-tune and (in both senses of the word) appreciate their learning.

I don't want to sugarcoat the process, though. In my experience, evaluating and grading form the most burdensome part of teaching. By the time I've finished fifty essays, my stamina and morale have been stretched thin. Alas, I have no magical labor-saving device to pull out of the pedagogical toolbox. But here are three options that will reduce your wear and tear.

(1) *You need not read every assignment.* Students should write to learn, and they don't necessarily depend on your affidavit to reach that goal. Similar to the suggestion for in-class quizzes, you can ask students to form partnerships and critique each other's answers to short-essay questions. Via this *pair and share* process, they will take responsibility for their own learning. If you or they

also want to award credit, you can collect the essays and give a grade of "complete."

(2) *You can evaluate every assignment, but not all at once.* This option applies best to more personalized types of writings such as response papers or journal entries. Because learning develops incrementally, students should complete these writings on schedule. Ideally you would maintain a dialogue by writing comments each time. Amid the doleful reality of too many students and too few hours, however, you can resort to a compromise. Rather than cutting back on the writings, ration your effort by collecting several assignments at a time. You will gain the double advantage of seeing a longer slice of each student's thinking while consolidating your replies.

Enforcement is also part of the doleful reality. How will you guarantee that students do each writing when they're supposed to? Here you may invoke your policing power. Announce that you will collect the assignments from different students every few weeks on a random basis.

(3) *You can use a checklist.* If you want to evaluate and grade every assignment, contemplate a checklist to expedite the task. At first glance, this may seem a strange idea; after all, students write in such individualized fashion. Basically, though, they are practicing standard expository skills and committing predictable mistakes. Even as you tailor your response to each essay, starting from scratch again and again, you're essentially repeating one or another type of critique. Therefore, some professors have devised checklists. Here are two models, one terse and the other loquacious.

Robert Weir has compiled a two-column list of a dozen standard features of expository writing (thesis, argument, documentation, etc.). The left-hand column describes each feature in positive terms ("well-stated argument"), the right-hand column in negative terms ("need deeper analysis"). After reading an essay, the teacher writes comments about notable substantive matters but simply marks the appropriate blanks in the checklist to evaluate mechanical matters. By using this checklist in conjunction with conferences and second drafts, Weir says he has not only improved students' skills but also cut his grading time by more than one-third.[9]

If you prefer a more detailed checklist, consider the set of "grading macros" developed by Lex Newman. With a single keystroke, he prints out whichever item(s) apply to students' first drafts. Given this feedback, students perform a series of exercises with TAS to clarify their writing. Here are two examples from the full array of "macros."

For paragraphing problems: Your paragraphing needs some work. Each paragraph should read like a mini essay, in which you state (very early in the paragraph) a *topic sentence* (i.e., something akin to a thesis statement of the paragraph). Then, as you shift subjects/topics, you should likewise shift paragraphs—taking care (again) to provide your reader with a new topic sentence. Some paragraphs will be long; others will be short. And that's fine. The length of a paragraph is not important; its focus is.

When the student relies on mere assertion versus argument: You're often confusing *assertion* with *argument*. It is one thing for someone to pound her fist and say/assert that, e.g., "capital punishment is wrong"; it is quite another thing to provide a line of reasoning as to why it is wrong. You often give unsupported assertions rather than providing a line of reasoning. For an example of this, see your page . . .[10]

BEING EVALUATED AND GRADED

You wield the power of the grade, but your classroom is not a monarchy. Your subjects will vote on your performance when they write course evaluations at the end (and perhaps also the middle) of the semester. To be sure, their opinions don't directly determine your job; academe isn't a democracy. Indirectly, however, their evaluations will exert some effect because, in most colleges and universities, they will be read by your department

Figure 8.3. Quantified Evaluation Form

1	2	3	4	5
poor	below average	average	above average	excellent

The quality of the lectures _____

The extent to which you found discussions useful _____

Overall rating of the instructor's teaching skill _____

chair, the promotion committee, and—if you go back on the job market—search committees elsewhere.

More immediately, they will be read by you and can serve your interests. Your attitude is the key. If you believe that good teachers aren't born but develop gradually through practice, advice, and self-reflection, then you will welcome student evaluations as reports by those who know your teaching best.

But, of course, it's not that simple. Three caveats:

(1) You will receive only what you ask for. As with public opinion polls, the wording of the question shapes the answers.

Many departments employ a multiple-choice, quantifiable form that itemizes a dozen or more behaviors and asks students to rate them. See Figure 8.3, for example. This "instrument" has the advantage of diagnosing specific aspects of your teaching. It also produces numerical scores that allow you and your chair to draw comparisons to your colleagues' performance.

On the other hand, in my experience the multiple-choice questionnaire doesn't tell teachers enough of what they want or need to know about themselves. It provides a grade more than an evaluation. So I recommend that you also use or create an evaluation form that invites students to respond in their own words.

Focused questions or directives ensure that you hear about certain issues. For example:

- In what ways have the lectures satisfied you? In what ways have they not?

- Please comment on the readings with regard to length, difficulty, and interest.
- Would you recommend this course to friends? Why or why not?

Better yet, lead off with a pair of wide-open questions, which will tap what's on students' minds rather than on yours:

- What were the merits of this course?
- What were the shortcomings of this course?[11]

(2) A few pages ago I encouraged you to welcome student evaluations. Now I hasten to add a consumer warning about side effects. First of all, student evaluations often inspire dread. As a social work professor recalls, "My first year of teaching, I was so anxious about my evaluations that I took them home unopened and locked myself in the bathroom before I looked inside the package."[12] And when you've dared to read them, what then? Probably you will be pleasantly surprised by the majority of comments: "awesome lectures"; "I never thought I'd enjoy macroeconomics"; "great discussions." Just as probably, though, you will feel wounded by the negative ones: "grading was ridiculously harsh"; "boring lectures"; "discussions meandered—a waste of time." If you're normal, you may obsess on these latter comments with varying degrees of self-deprecation and vengefulness, second-guessing everything you did during the semester while suspecting those two guys in the back row as your malevolent critics.

At this point, some reality testing will be in order. Call upon a trusted friend to read the evaluations and give his or her impression. Invariably, your friend will find them far more positive than you have. Last year, for example, I sank into despair after skimming through the final evaluations of my favorite course. Students reported being confused, bored, even alienated. What had gone awry? I brooded. What should I have done? Finally, my wife asked, "How many students are you talking about?" I reread the eighty-five evaluations, dividing them into "positive," "generally positive," and "negative" piles, and discovered that the third pile totaled exactly seven.

One can hardly ask for a better batting average. Remember Ted

Williams, who in 1941 was the last baseball player to hit over .400. That was an extraordinary feat. But he also failed to get on base 60 percent of the time.

Or as one of my colleagues liked to remark, even Jesus lost one out of twelve.

(3) For my third caveat, let's step back and emphasize that successful teaching is not a popularity contest. In the dialogic relationship with students, you are seeking to challenge and extend their thinking, not merely to entertain or reassure them. You hope to take them beyond their "comfort zone" into territory where they will question their mental model and ponder new, disturbing possibilities. As Socrates found out, that kind of teaching doesn't necessarily win friendly reviews.

Indeed, some critics claim that student evaluations violate the best purposes of education. "Most of all I dislike the attitude of calm consumer expertise that pervades the responses," argues Mark Edmundson, an English professor at the University of Virginia. "I'm disturbed by the serene belief that my function—and, more important, Freud's, or Shakespeare's, or Blake's—is to divert, entertain, and interest." That belief, he claims, reflects university culture, which in turn reflects American culture at large: namely, that students are to "enjoy" a course rather than be challenged and changed by it.[13]

The fact is, however, that most students enjoy being challenged. They rate hard courses and tough graders more positively than "slide courses" because they value the challenge of high intellectual standards.[14] To earn their appreciation you need not pander or put on a performance. Nor do you need to hand out "A"s. Yes, higher ratings are correlated with higher grades, but that's usually because those teachers were more effective. To quote one education scholar's synopsis of numerous studies: "Students of highly rated teachers achieve higher final exam scores, can better apply course material, and are more inclined to pursue the subject subsequently."[15] As noted in chapter 1, students applaud teachers who are enthusiastic, lucid, and organized and who treat them fairly as well as caringly.

Students are not equipped, however, to evaluate the *content* of your teaching. They are novices in your field, after all. For this reason, I encourage you to seek advice from your peers. Ask a colleague to read your evaluations and assess them according to his or her experience. Or go a step further: invite a colleague to visit your classroom. Being observed may be somewhat disquieting, but it gives you a unique opportunity. Instead of leaving class and trying to replay the lecture or discussion in your mind, you can talk about it with a fellow teacher—an eyewitness.

Moreover, you can equalize the relationship and double the benefits by offering to visit his or her class in return. If all goes well, ask your visitor to write a report, which will form a significant addition to your teaching portfolio. This person need not be in your field, by the way. The crucial criteria are that you respect his or her teaching ability and that you trust him or her.

You may be fortunate enough to be on a campus that has a Teaching and Learning Center. If so, you can ask the consultants there to interpret your evaluations, observe a class, or coach you in other ways. The advantages are twofold. Not only will you be working with pedagogical experts; they won't be voting on your promotion.

If for some reason you don't invite an observer to your classroom, you will benefit by observing yourself via videotape. But be prepared for what you'll see—or rather, what you won't see. A camera, even in the hands of a skilled operator, can't fully reproduce the quality and "feel" of what took place. You're watching a twenty-one-inch version, with none of the usual flair of a television show. Worse, you're seeing and hearing yourself ("do I really smile like *that?*" "does my voice sound like *that?*"). So I repeat the recommendation made for student evaluations: ask a friend to sit beside you and provide reality testing. With his or her help you will gain pointers about how effectively you speak, how you respond to students' comments, and whether you have distracting mannerisms.

Appendix 8.1:
Teaching through Comments on Students' Papers

(1) Read through the entire paper without marking it. While reading, try not to measure the essay against a template in your mind. Even though it's hard to do after the fifteenth or twenty-sixth answer to the same question, put yourself in the author's mind and figure out what he/she is trying to say.

(2) Identify what the author has done well. How can his/her strengths be used to repair weaknesses?

(3) Identify the one or two most important problems—that is, the problems that are most worth teaching the author to overcome. Now you are ready to begin marking the paper.

(4) Questions can help call attention to trouble spots, but avoid questions that can be answered simply "yes" or "no." The student will dismiss them too easily. Preface questions with *why*, *how*, or *what* so that the student must reexamine the paper and become self-critical.

(5) Avoid labeling problems unless you also give the author a way of overcoming them. Instead of saying "confusing" (which doesn't help the author know how you are confused), write "Do you mean ... or ... ?" or "Sorry, I get lost in this long sentence" or "But on p. 3 you said Lincoln hated war."

(6) Use praise not simply as "feel good" commentary but to help the author learn. Always follow "good" or "I like this" with "*because* . . . ." Another way of saying this is: Let your marginal comments express your responses as you accompany the author through his/her essay. This will be difficult at first, but you'll gradually get the hang of it.

(7) Avoid doing the student's work. It's tempting to correct errors or rewrite poor prose. But the author will simply nod in agreement or, perhaps, feel violated. If you want the student to learn how to recognize and correct a problem, you must ask him/her to make the change. If you do, however, you should be dealing with a significant or chronic problem—not merely misspelling "Roosevelt" or misdating the War of 1812.

(8) Minimize comments in the margins, particularly negative ones. Confronting a page covered with scribbles, an occasional student may be grateful for your attention, but most students will feel overwhelmed and despairing.

Focus the student's attention (and save your energy) by putting most of your comments into a succinct, carefully thought-out response at the end.

Frame it as a letter from you to the author, addressing the student by name. Write two paragraphs. In paragraph 1, describe what the student has done well. In paragraph 2, describe the essay's one or two major weaknesses. Why are these weaknesses an obstacle for the reader? What specific activities will help the student overcome the weaknesses next time?

Be kind. Assume the student has tried his/her best and fearfully awaits your response to his/her creation. (In this regard, note that I shifted from addressing "the student" in the positive paragraph to addressing "the essay" in the negative paragraph.)

Compare the following comments at the end of two students' essays:

Lydia: This essay has some good ideas, but they aren't very clear. You didn't spend enough time organizing them or finding evidence to support them. Commas and spelling need work, too. You consistently misspell "secession."
Thomas

Allen: You have produced a lucid and interesting explanation of the Civil War. I particularly like the examples you cite on page 2 because they clarify the importance of John Brown and "fanaticism" in pushing the South to secede. (By the way, it's "secede," not "succeed.")

The essay would be stronger if it had said more about Lincoln's policy toward slavery. On page 3 you say "he hated it," but that doesn't clarify what he proposed to *do* about it. Do you see how there's a missing link in the story? Moreover, the thesis paragraph doesn't do justice to the rest of your essay. It repeats the question instead of alerting the reader to your subsequent argument (which you capsulize neatly in your conclusion).

I'll be glad to talk about this.

Thomas

(9) Write a note to yourself about the student's main achievement and main problem(s). Or make a copy of your comments. This will enable you to chart the student's progress next time.

Evaluating essays is a difficult skill. But the more you practice, the better and faster you will perform it.[16]

Appendix 8.2: A Detailed Rubric

Organization: Does the introduction provide a clear thesis statement? Is it obvious, in the opening paragraph, where the paper will be going and how it will get there? Does the body of the paper follow the argument and outline established in the introduction? Does the conclusion succinctly tie together the main argument? Does the paper meet the length requirement of the assignment?

Analysis: Does the paper get to the main point immediately? Does it avoid extraneous background or summary information? Does the paper offer insightful observations and connections that demonstrate a thorough understanding of the text? Does the paper address all parts of the question?

Style: Is the paper well written and easy to read? Does it have paragraphs that begin with clear topic sentences? Are paragraphs connected with smooth transitional sentences? Does each paragraph convey one clear point? Does the paper contain grammatical errors or spelling mistakes? Does it avoid the passive voice, convoluted words and phrases, and overly lengthy sentences and paragraphs?

Evidence: Does the paper offer well-chosen, relevant material that effectively supports the thesis? Does it provide a convincing, insightful interpretation of this evidence? Does the choice of evidence demonstrate a firm command of the entire text, not just one part?[17]

Appendix 8.3: A Quantitative Rubric

Student: _____
Paper: _____

Criterion	Possible	Normal	Yours
1. Paper has a clear focus that fits well into the course.	4.5	3.5	____
2. The argument is well structured.	4.5	3.5	____
3. The paper represents a suitable amount of work. The argument is of sufficient depth and detail.	6.0	4.5	____
4. The author correctly employs concepts used in the course.	6.0	3.5	____
5. The author uses appropriate sources. The author shows an understanding of the literature and uses it in an appropriate way to support the paper.	4.5	3.5	____
6. The paper is well written from the point of view of grammar, style, and spelling.	4.5	3.5	____
Total	30	23	____[18]

Extracurriculars

part Three

9 / Relating to Students

During his freshman year at the University of Texas at Austin, Willie Morris—newly arrived from rural Yazoo City, Mississippi—was invited to the apartment of a young graduate student and his wife.

The walls of their apartment were lined with books, more books than I had ever seen before in a private dwelling—books everywhere and on everything. I was astonished; I tried to talk with those people, but I was unaccountably shy, and I kept looking at their books out of the corner of my eye, and wondering if I should *say* something about them, or ask perhaps if they were for sale or if they formed some kind of special exhibit. It is a rare experience for certain young people to see great quantities of books in a private habitat for the first time, and to hear ideas talked about seriously in the off hours. Good God, they were doing it for pleasure, or so it seemed. The wife, who was also a graduate student, asked me what I wanted to do with myself when I graduated from college. "I want to be a writer," I said, but not even thinking about it until the words were out; my reply surprised me most of all.[1]

In the years to come, Morris would be a Rhodes Scholar, editor of the *Texas Observer* and then *Harper's Magazine,* and author of numerous books.

The epiphany that teachers hope to ignite is not the proverbial lightbulb. It is more like a candle that they struggle to light—and then keep lit—amid the breezy yawns in classrooms and the gusts of campus life. But even this metaphor doesn't capture the mystery of how a student becomes inspired with curiosity or insight.

Sometimes it occurs without apparent effort or design, in an ostensibly unpedagogical occasion that imprints more profoundly than any lesson plan.

Most of the time, you meet your students in the classroom and vicariously in the reading and writing assignments. That is where you do most of your work, putting into play the purposes and strategies that we've discussed up to now. Occasionally, however, the most powerful teaching takes place outside those venues: on a campus bench, or in your office, or across the table of a coffee house, or after class without you but nonetheless because of you. This aspect of the teaching/learning dialogic is unscripted, more personalized, and governed by looser rules. Not only will it reinforce your curricular goals. It also may produce meanings that go deeper and last longer: an "aha!" or even, as in Willie Morris's case, a transformation.

This chapter will sketch various extracurricular formats for interaction with your students, discussing the opportunities, as well as the pitfalls.

By now it's hard to remember how students contacted instructors before the era of e-mail. The messages land in your electronic mailbox at any hour of day or night, depositing requests, problems, queries, essays, something that demands your attention. "Hi Professor. I'm in your Econ 101 but was absent this morning because my car had a flat so I need to make up the quiz. I'm really sorry. Carl Costas." This one-to-one communication is not exactly person-to-person. If there are eighty students in the class, you probably won't know which one is Carl Costas. And even if you can identify him, you will struggle to read between these few hasty lines to assess his attitude (is he sorrier about the car or the quiz?). In the pre-Internet era, he would have come to your office or talked with you at the next class. Now you're engaging in an administrative transaction rather than a relationship.

On the other hand, the very ease and impersonality of e-mail sometimes invites students to say what they wouldn't say face-to-face "Professor Smith: You may have noticed I've been absent all week, but I hope you'll forgive me. The reason is my roommate tried to commit suicide on Sunday and I've stayed with him and his parents in the hospital."

E-mail oils the wheels of communication with superb efficiency, but the relationship remains abstract: words on a screen to and from an invisible person. As soon as the student walks into your room, however, you have more to work with. You can read body language, gauge tone of voice, exchange words immediately (not mediated), and share a laugh. The two of you join in a teaching/learning dialogue that is personalized, by addressing this student's particular needs, and therefore is more likely to take effect.

"Hi, Carolyn. What can I do for you?"

She holds out her midterm essay like a used towel, and you glimpse the "C-plus" at the end of your typed comments. "I don't understand where I went wrong," she says.

You thought you had explained it clearly in your comments, but obviously not. So now, with the author in the room, you redirect the dialogue. "Tell me how you began studying."

"Well, I read Tumin's article on social stratification three times," she says, pointing to her xeroxed copy, where almost every line glows with yellow highlighter. "But I kept getting lost. You see, I'm a biology major, and this is my first Soc. course."

You align your chair beside hers and say, "Let's figure this out together." You hand her a green highlighter pen and ask a series of leading questions. "What's the most important sentence in a paragraph? What's the most important paragraph in an article? If you wanted to find an author's 'thesis,' where in the article should you look first?"

Eventually, she turns to you with a smile. "I get it. I missed the green forest because I was too busy marking every tree. Thanks."

She leaves your office clutching the green highlighter that you gave her as a souvenir, armed with a new strategy for learning. You lean back in your chair, reflecting upon how teaching sometimes succeeds and sometimes doesn't. You had given two lectures about social stratification and had written two lengthy paragraphs on Carolyn's essay, but only now has she figured out how to understand the topic. Lecturing to all those expressionless faces behind which so many students hide is a little like sending out e-mail: you always wonder whether they're reading you. After this twenty-minute one-to-one lesson, you know for sure.

But that's not all of the reward. As mentioned so often, the learning goes two ways. For example, as you reflect upon Carolyn's confusion, you realize how your lectures should have drawn a link to Tumin's article. And since your leading questions proved so helpful to her, you prepare a handout for all students on "How to Find the Forest among the Trees of Your Reading."

The trouble is, few students will visit your office. "Please feel free to come and chat during my office hours," you proclaimed in your syllabus. "I'm always happy to meet students." But week after week you sit alone, except during those two days before an exam when anxious students line up in the hall. Don't fault yourself or your students. After all, how often have you visited your physician just to talk? One goes to the doctor when something hurts, hoping to leave as soon as possible with a remedy.

How can you win more visitors? You might go beyond simply announcing office hours and, instead, circulate appointment sheets in class every week, inviting students to "come by for twenty minutes so we can get to know each other." In my experience, several will take the bait. Once they do, you can put them at ease with chitchat about your dog Annie or a trip to Montana, opening the way for more substantive, intellectual exchange. Even if a conversation stays chatty, though, the gulf between teacher and student will have narrowed; the relationship will have thickened. As a result, students will feel more trusting, speak up more often in class, and be more likely to revisit your office hours. You, in turn, will feel that much more connected to the class.

Or you can move office hours outside the office. Instead of opening the door and waiting for students to walk in, go out to the students. Tell them that, during this week's office hours, you'll be drinking coffee at "The Daily Grind" in the quad or eating lunch in the campus cafeteria. Or, if you have a small enough class, invite them for dinner at your house or apartment, which will humanize the learning experience.

Derrick Bell, New York University professor of constitutional law, goes further. "My challenge," he explains, "is structuring courses that give [students] a chance to teach one another, both the course material and their life perspectives." To achieve his curricular goal, he requires them to work together in teams of three or four to argue a case before the entire class, which acts as a giant court, debating and finally "handing down" its decision. With an eye toward the extracurricular horizon, at the end of each class Bell takes the day's team to a little Italian restaurant in Greenwich Village. Over dinner he talks about his life and asks about theirs, engaging in a conversation that touches on their hopes, ideas, anxieties, ambitions. It's an evening that none of those students will ever forget.[2]

In time or money you probably can't afford Italian restaurants. More important, you may not want to invest or disclose so much of yourself in relationships with students. As was emphasized in chapter 1, every teacher should stay true to his or her own personality and values. You may prefer to work within the boundaries of your office, concentrating on academic rather than personal matters.

Wherever you place yourself on the extracurricular continuum, though, you will face a variety of challenges. Some students will use your office to lobby for a higher grade. Some will want to be your friend. Some will look to you as a counselor for their personal problems. Each conversation offers you an opportunity for a kind of teaching that extends far beyond the subject matter of your course. And each entails a risk.

When a student tells you in a shaky voice that "I worked all night on the essay but I got a B-minus and I really need an A in this course," you not only can discuss the exam. You can also discuss better writing strategies, ask how he/she is faring in other courses, and (depending on his or her willingness, and yours) inquire what or who is pressuring him to "need" an "A." With these latter questions, you may produce insights that are deeper and more lasting than that essay. On the other hand, be aware of a certain risk. By working intensively with a student, you may develop a personal stake that skews your evaluation of his/her next essay. This essay is no better than the previous one and, in frustration, you give it a lower grade than it deserves; or on the other hand, you give it a higher grade because you empathize with the author.

You may also risk blurring or overstepping teacher-student boundaries. Whether or not your campus has instituted a sexual harassment policy, you need to be self-conscious about your behavior. Perhaps needless to say, don't date your students. The discrepancy between your power and theirs automatically makes such a relationship inappropriate. Students can harbor misguided motives for and notions about their relationship with a faculty member. On a more mundane level, keep your office door open when talking with students.

But what about having a personal conversation with a student who says that a paper is still only half-done because his/her parents are getting divorced and he/she is too upset to work? I certainly hope you will engage in a compassionate discussion. Suppose, however, that at the end the student squeezes your hand and says, "This was great. Let's do it again." Now you need to consider your response scrupulously. Even though you want to show that you care, you need to retain that small reserve that marks a professional relationship. As teachers we can talk with our students about the personal part of our lives, but not the private. The line between friendliness and friendship is ambiguous, yet real.[3]

So is the line between teacher and therapist. Despite an understandable impulse to deal with this student's psychological situation, you will be more helpful by referring him or her to a professional counselor. "Have you found anyone to talk to about your feelings?" you ask.

"Well, my girlfriend's been helpful and understanding and all."

"Good. But that's asking a lot of her. I know several students in crisis who got excellent help from the counselors at the Student Health Service. I hope you'll consider talking with one of them." (You might even write down the phone number and, if you know it, the name of someone to see.)

On the other hand, when students come to you with "life issues," you have the opportunity for truly significant teaching. There's the student who is being pushed by his/her parents to be a doctor, but who wants to be an artist. Or another one who can't figure out how to balance political activism and academic work. These quandaries belong properly to the professor's role.[4]

Even if you succeed in drawing an appropriate boundary line, however, you run a final risk. In the zeal to inspire, help, and care for your students, after a while you are no longer lighting candles. You are burning out. But let's deal with that problem in the next chapter, which will outline survival strategies.

I wouldn't be a responsible teacher if I didn't mention the pitfalls of extracurricular relations with students. On balance, however, I believe that the benefits outweigh the risks. Indeed, some of my most effective teaching has taken place during interactions outside the classroom. I gratefully recall, for example, one student's remark at the end of an intense conversation about the second draft of her honors paper. "It's amazing," she said, "how I leave your office discovering that I have ideas I didn't know I had when I walked in here." And then there was the postcard from Guatemala: "Working with the people here is just what I dreamed of. Thanks for helping me decide."

10 / Teaching and not Perishing

It's not the same as a robber shouting "your money or your life!" But among untenured faculty the warning to "publish or perish" arouses a comparable sense of dread. According to the standard formula, unless you produce a book or at least several articles in scholarly journals within six years, all your work and hopes for a career will be shot down. If that's the prescription for success, one has to wonder how much effort a new instructor should put into teaching. Does it make sense to emulate your inspirational professor (as recommended in chapter 1) and maybe win an award for excellent teaching, only to be told, "Sorry, but we only grant tenure to scholars"?

Like most interesting questions, this one has a complicated answer—or really a set of answers, each starting with "It all depends." This concluding chapter will sketch some of the sobering realities that subordinate teaching. At the same time, we will discover reasons that good teaching counts a lot. To a surprising extent, in fact, the appropriate adage is "teach or perish."

When he was asked about the relative weight given to teaching versus publication in the tenure process, the Harvard paleontologist Stephen Jay Gould replied, "To be perfectly honest, though lip service is given to teaching, I have never seriously heard teaching considered in any meeting for promotion. I do not subscribe to any overly romanticized notion that teaching is primary or that tenure should be awarded only on teaching." His colleague in Harvard's Department of Social Relations, Daniel Bell, echoed that view: "I do not think teaching ought to be the primary criterion of tenure or scholarship at a great university."[1]

Nothing is ambiguous about these answers. At research universities like Harvard there are many admirable teachers, but in the final reckoning everyone will be measured by their publications.

We need to keep a sense of perspective, though. The Harvards, Yales, and Stanfords constitute only a small minority of the academic world, 60 out of 4,000 institutions of higher education.[2] If you're hired by one of these other 3,940 places, the expectations will differ considerably, sometimes radically. At Pitzer College in Claremont, California, for example, a sociologist explains that "by law . . . you get evaluated on the basis of four criteria, listed in descending order of priorities. . . . If you don't meet the first one, it stops right there. There will be no contract. That first criterion is teaching and advising. . . . The second one is something we call 'contribution to the college as an intellectual community.' What that means is that you need to be involved in collegial things."[3] In other schools of varying sizes and prestige—Mills College, for example, or the University of South Dakota, or DePauw University—faculty say the same: "Quality teaching. That's the one thing that if you don't do, you will not get tenure. . . ."[4]

So far as I can judge, the large majority of colleges and universities fit somewhere between these two poles, giving weight to both teaching and publishing. But exactly how much weight? That depends on not only where you work, but when. "In the past[,] sociology was primarily a teaching department, although research was done," reports a longtime professor at Oregon State University. "Now research has become much, much more important. I have a certain amount of frustration with that[,] given that I think really good teaching is pretty much a full-time job. . . . I'm teaching two courses per quarter with 60 students in one and 80 students in the other."[5] According to one of the numerous assistant professors who have been journeymen from one nontenured job to another, only small private colleges—denominational, black, and women's colleges—reward good teaching.[6]

At all too many institutions, unfortunately, the ground rules are ambiguous. "You could not get tenure here [San Jose State University] without publishing," Wendy Ng reports, "although I do think you could get tenure with having mediocre teaching evaluations and publishing. See what I mean, even though they say teaching is number one?"[7] Each year, one hears stories of junior faculty who won a teaching award and soon afterward were turned down for tenure.[8] Given these mixed signals, should one spend the weekend designing a creative class or researching an article? At many colleges the answer seems to be "do both." The same Mills College professor who stated that quality teaching was the sine qua non for tenure went on to lament, "And yet, even though we are teachers, we're also scholars. I feel as though we have to be doing some research, not every single day, but certainly every year. . . . If you don't publish at all, they will get rid of you. . . . They give lip service to teaching, and they will fire you if you don't teach well, but they do not give you the environment in which to do it. Woo! Sorry about that."[9]

It's a juggling act, in other words, to be performed under adverse circumstances. In fact, academics typically have to learn how to keep not merely these two balls in the air, but three: teaching, publication, and community service. Colleges and universities depend upon enormous amounts of volunteer work by faculty, most of which is invisible—department committees, campuswide committees, search committees, advising, lunches with prospective students, dinners with prospective faculty. According to the U.S. Department of Education, full-time faculty typically spend eleven hours per week on administrative and service tasks, which is three hours more than they spend in the classroom.[10]

Ideally, you'll be exempted from such assignments during your first year or two, so that you can concentrate on your courses and become acclimated to your new environment. But there's no guarantee of that luxury, particularly if you're female and/or an ethnic minority. As colleges promote gender equality and cultural diversity, women, African Americans, and Asian Americans are besieged with appeals to serve on this or that committee and give speeches to student or alumni groups. "I've been to [i.e., taught at] six different universities," declares a tenure-track professor at Indiana University, Kokomo, "and I don't believe the ideology that the students come first. I am not convinced that any of them really mean that. They still hang on to the old values of publish or perish. They still have so many service expectations, especially for women."[11]

Can you say "no" to requests for service? Again the answer is "it depends." As a newcomer, you won't know whom you can safely refuse or whom you shouldn't displease. Each department has its unique politics. Seek out trustworthy consultants, not only people who have worked in the institution for years, but junior members who have recently been in your situation. One first-year instructor, for instance, learned about some informal rules: wear a tie and jacket; listen, don't talk, in department meetings.[12] In the course of asking about campus politics and mores, you'll make some friends and, with luck, may even find a mentor.[13]

One thing you can be sure of, though: you will hit the ground running. "First-semester professing is turning out to be far more hectic than last-semester grad-schooling," a new instructor reported from Kutztown University in Pennsylvania. "But I'm getting paid for it!"[14] The Department of Education estimates a fifty-two-hour work week for full-time faculty (including eight hours for teaching and nineteen for class preparation), but newcomers will probably exceed that.[15] You not only will be keeping up with a three- or four-course teaching load, holding office hours, and attending department meetings. You will also be taking care of laundry, groceries, and other mundane matters. "In my first year of teaching," Professor Penny Gold recalled twenty-six years later, "I did little besides prepare for class, eat, sleep (not enough), and bring my new 'lemon' car in for repairs."[16]

Nevertheless, let's hope you will sustain a semblance of private life. Eat lunch with colleagues, see a movie, work out at the gym. Family, friends and recreation are crucial to emotional and physical health. After all, your sense of well-being is nourished by gratifications beyond the classroom. Or, as one of my senior colleagues remarked, "no matter how hard you work, your chairman will never say 'I love you.'"

I promised sobering realities, and I have delivered that promise—perhaps too well. Teaching several new courses is hard. Teaching them well is harder yet. Teaching well amid the other demands of academe may sound impossible, so that now, in the last chapter, I risk leaving you overwhelmed. In other words, if this were all to be said, I would be defeating the purposes of this guidebook.

Fortunately, there is also encouraging news. In navigating the sink-or-swim rapids of life before tenure, teaching is not only your "load" but also your lifesaver.[17] Even as Nancy Greenwood vehemently complained about the unreasonable workload at Indiana University, Kokomo, for example, she also said, "For me teaching is still the place I know I get intrinsic benefits. I can have a crummy day with my kid. I can have a crummy day with my colleagues. But I can go into the classroom and most of the time leave and feel like I've done something good that day."[18]

Perhaps it will be when the hitherto silent student in the back row stops you after class to ask, "What can I read about that guy Albert Camus you quoted today?" Or maybe it will happen halfway through your lecture when, to your surprise, you find yourself illustrating the neopluralist theory of interest groups in terms of a recent episode on campus. Or it could be the animated argument among break-out groups that went on for five minutes beyond the hour. This experience of making an impact on others— of nurturing curiosity, insight, and, yes, pleasure—this is what will buoy you even as you hurry home to that pile of fifty-five blue books waiting on your desk. I have written this book to help you enjoy such moments.

But how can you accomplish these moments while carrying a load of a hundred or more students in three or four courses? In the long run, exhaustion trumps enthusiasm and pedagogical skill. So let me recommend two kinds of shortcuts, each of which will expedite your work without compromising your principles.

DON'T BE A PERFECTIONIST

In graduate school you may have already learned that the quest for a perfect dissertation was counterproductive. Despite all those page-long footnotes and that polished prose, your committee recommended numerous revisions before you submit it to a publisher for yet more suggested changes. After all, there are two types of dissertations: perfect and completed. The same lesson applies to your first year of teaching. For one thing, you won't have the leisure to reflect and perfect. When classes begin, the stream of consciousness turns into a muddy torrent. More basically, your courses will be perpetual works-in-progress—drafts by which you learn what to add or revise for the next time and the time after that.

Furthermore, don't aim to enrich every lecture and discussion with original ideas. In more ways than one, originality is inappropriate. Not only will you lack the time for such research and thinking. You also will be teaching one or more courses outside your field of expertise, so you will be learning on the run. Most important, as explained in chapter 5, a class is not the same as a scholarly meeting or graduate seminar. The lecture that impresses your colleagues will fly over your students' heads. The most effective presentation conveys no more than two central ideas—ones that you find familiar or even clichés but that will be news to most of your undergraduates. So take advantage of the hard work already done by predecessors. As suggested earlier, open three textbooks, general studies, and/or notes from a course you took in college. Borrow liberally from their material, framing it within the questions and goals of your own course.

The same antiperfectionist advice applies to other aspects of teachings—writing assignments, for example. Chapter 8 discussed strategies for asking students to write frequently without crushing you under an avalanche of paper. Here let's focus not on evaluation and grading, but on the scope of the assignments. In an ideal learning environment, one would invite students to write essays on topics of their own choosing—personal explorations rather than a one-route-fits-all approach. In reality, that requires an instructor to supervise fifty or a hundred novices exploring in myriad directions. To ensure that they return with a completed essay, you need to help each of them define a feasible topic, devise significant questions, locate useful sources, and so on. Narrowing their choices to a few predefined topics won't simply preserve your sanity. It will enhance your students' success.

Similarly, don't apologize for creating a less-than-state-of-the-art Web page for your course, or even for doing without one. It would be wonderful to offer your students a Web page deftly laid out, glowing with colorful images, structured around several menus, studded with links to interesting sites, and furnishing a forum for discussions among you and students. But that is icing on the curricular cake. First come the various pedagogical tasks that have occupied us in the preceding chapters: defining your aims and outcomes, constructing the syllabus, writing lectures, and planning discussions as well as other learning activities. Unless you perform these effectively, even the most exquisite Web page won't compensate. A syllabus is only as good as the ideas that go into it.

Employ the same modesty when incorporating technology into your classroom. College students today have come of age with PowerPoint, the Web, DVDs, and VCRs. They download photos, burn CDs, and shoot and edit videos without a qualm. For them—and perhaps for you, too—slides and audiotapes are old-fashioned, and overhead transparencies are quaint. Increasingly, students expect high production values in classroom presentations, and you will be tempted to satisfy them. In the long run, that is the right direction. Technology can be a powerful ally not simply in arousing students' interest but, beyond entertainment, in stimulating their understanding and creativity. As mentioned in chapters 5 and 7, when a teacher works through more than one sensory channel—auditory as well as visual—he/she satisfies a diversity of learning styles. And with the limitless resources out there on the World Wide Web, with a few clicks of the mouse one can import extraordinary images or texts into your classroom. Imagine the responses you will evoke from your students with a PowerPoint presentation about the English slave trade that juxtaposes pictures of a slave ship and a space ship, then projects a Cruikshank cartoon while playing an African song, and finally reproduces from a Liverpool website a list of eighteenth-century slave traders.[19]

Such exciting, elegant technique is hard to resist. But it is only a means—a medium for teaching. Technology does not necessarily add up to pedagogy. The question is: how will you use it to promote learning? Paradoxically, a powerful high-tech presentation may induce students to sit back as passive consumers.[20]

There are also practical caveats. How much production time will a sophisticated PowerPoint presentation require? Create one or two presentations, then multiply the hours by the number of classes in your schedule. Also keep in mind the adage that everything will take longer than it's supposed to. And, oh yes, find out whether your classrooms are wired for laptop computers and Internet. Even if they are, the dire possibility remains that after all your hard work and with your students ready and watching, you'll push the button and nothing will happen. The revenge of modern technology! Then what will you do? It's always a good idea to be prepared with a backup.

You have a long career ahead of you, let's hope. Concentrate more on the course than on the Web page. Be content with a few audiovisual productions this year, and a few more in each year to come. Meanwhile, you can be a splendid teacher (though less glitzy) by relying on a xeroxed syllabus, chalkboard, overhead projector, slide projector, and a vcr. The best computer ever invented, after all, is the human brain.

DON'T GIVE YOURSELF AWAY

Students rate most highly those teachers who are enthusiastic and caring. Correspondingly, teachers who strive for excellence will devote extraordinary energy and time to their students. But here, too, one must beware of the quicksand of perfectionism. In the fluid realm of ideas, enough easily seems not good enough. Just as a lecture or discussion can always be improved, students' understanding can be deepened, their enthusiasm raised, their writings strengthened. So you add a few office hours, invite students to have coffee with you, encourage them to e-mail questions or problems, give them your home telephone number for emergencies, and allow them to rewrite essays. The response is gratifying. You're holding countless conversations outside of class, reading numerous second drafts, answering a dozen e-mail messages per day. A student phones at midnight and says, "I need to talk with you tomorrow, but I can't make your office hours," so you agree to meet her at 10 A.M., although you had planned to grade exams in the morning.

In principle, all this is laudable. But to state the problem bluntly, there are more of them than there are of you. Before long, you risk being swallowed up by their enthusiasm and needs. In your dedication to what is on their minds, you don't pay enough attention to your own mind. Midway through the semester, you realize that you're so busy talking with, listening to, and counseling students that you have no time to think.

This danger exists even at a research university like the University of Iowa, where junior faculty teach only two courses. Listen to the painful testimony by sociologist Jodi O'Brien, Ph.D. '92.

In a typical day, I teach a couple of classes, meet with a couple of students for a fair amount of time carving through their dissertations. I maybe will have a committee meeting, and do the basic administrative stuff that always lands on the desk everyday. It can be a very full day, from 7 A.M. to 7 P.M., and there may even be a seminar at night. I found all these activities engaging and useful. Then this voice that never leaves me creeps through and says, "You didn't do any real work." . . .

I would say that voice dogs my generation of scholars teach[ing] in research institutions, and increasingly even in some of the teaching colleges. We have fewer resources than any generation of which I'm aware, and still we wish to publish and to meet the standards. I can't tell you how devastating it is to live with that voice on an on-going basis. I've spent a lot of time thinking how I can shut that voice up, so that I won't end up in a state of depression.[21]

The remedy is commonsensical, although more easily preached than performed: namely, set limits.

- Even though you recognize the value of second drafts, you might restrict them to students who wrote papers of "C" or "D" quality.
- If you permit students to phone you at home, say "before 10 P.M."

- Three office hours per week will ordinarily suffice for students' needs. Indeed, most professors find themselves sitting alone except on the days before and after exams.
- In this e-mail era, when students fill your mailbox at all hours of day or night, you need not rush to your keyboard to reply. A few teachers have announced "virtual office hours," say from 2:00 to 3:00 P.M. on weekdays, as the only times they will answer e-mail. If such limits seem unduly narrow, at least explain to your students that you won't necessarily reply the same day.
- More fundamentally, remind yourself that you can't save every one of your students from confusion, stress, or incompetence. To harbor that expectation not only verges on grandiosity. It also skews the dialogic balance between teaching and learning. A successful teacher encourages students to develop autonomy and meet him or her halfway.

A bit of time saved here and a bit there will add up to a lot of time for nurturing your research and writing. To make the best use of it, try to carve out a bloc each week—say, Tuesday and Thursday mornings, and maybe the interval between semesters. Write your name on your calendar for an appointment with yourself.

Conclusion

Con-clude: v.t. To bring to an end; finish; terminate. [ME from
L *concludere*, to end an argument, var. of *claudere* to close.]
—*Random House Dictionary of the English Language* (1983)

How to conclude? I found this to be a surprisingly perplex-
ing question. After considerable reflection, I understand why. To
close this book would violate one of the principles that it has been
espousing. Teaching and learning should not "finish" or "terminate" at the end of a course or a year or a book about pedagogy.
(Indeed, after you teach a lecture or discussion, I picture you
scribbling notes to yourself, "Change this, keep that!" as you look
ahead to teaching it again.)

Not only that, if I were to "end the argument," I would be
contradicting an even more basic principle: namely, that teaching
entails a dialogue. Writing does the same. In each chapter I have
addressed you—invisible and inaudible though you are—while
trying to anticipate your questions and responses.

Moreover, how can I have the last word in this dialogue without seeming to win the argument? That kind of conclusion would
violate the premise that teachers have varied goals, values, and
personalities.

In the light of these reflections, I decided to conclude with a
half-dozen gentle reminders of the major aims of this book, followed by an invitation.

Actually, I have already delivered many of these reminders in
the preceding paragraphs.

- When you teach, you enter a relationship with students.
  Regardless of whether they are talking, listening, writing,
  or reading, you and they share an *interactive* process.

- In designing a course, you need to define both sides of this relationship: not only the subject matter (aims) but also how you want students to grasp the subject matter (outcomes).
- Teaching is only as successful as the learning it produces. Therefore, you will improve your effectiveness by frequently eliciting various kinds of feedback. The more you know about the mental models and cognitive skills that students bring to the course, the more successfully you will help those students attain your high standards.
- Excellent teaching is not the same as excellent scholarship. Your students are newcomers to your course and perhaps to your entire field. So they will have different interests than the ones that you have matured during years of graduate school. You needn't be brilliant to do your job well. The best teachers are enthusiastic, communicate ideas clearly, and treat students fairly.
- Finally, please be fair to yourself. Don't expect to produce a flawless course on the first or even the third attempt. That is a surefire recipe for disappointment. Teaching, like learning, improves by trial and error and reflection upon the error. It's about process, not product.

Meanwhile, don't sacrifice yourself to your course and students. Reserve time for personal well-being. Without friendships and family, solitude, and recreation, you won't bring whole-hearted and whole-minded zeal to your teaching.

Those are the reminders. Now for the invitation.

However much I would like to believe that these teachings will guarantee your success and joy, I know better. I have tossed out the Frisbee; now you do with it whatever suits your values, circumstances, and temperament. Like the best dialogues, however, I hope that this one continues to grow. In other words, please contact me to say how this guidebook has helped you through your first year and how it can perform that task better. Instead of saying goodbye, I say farewell and *au revoir*.

Notes

Introduction

1. My thanks to Lee Warren, Derek Bok Center for Teaching and Learning, Harvard University, for clarifying this point.

2. For the Frisbee metaphor, I thank Ed Neal, the University of North Carolina Center for Teaching and Learning.

Chapter One

1. Peter Seldin, *The Teaching Portfolio: A Practical Guide to Improved Performance and Promotion/Tenure Decisions* (Bolton, Mass.: Anker, 1991), 1; Thomas M. Sherman et al., "The Quest for Excellence in University Teaching," *Journal of Higher Education* 58 (January/February 1987): 66.

2. Sara Rimer, "The Rothschild Files," *New York Times Education Supplement*, January 5, 1992, 25.

3. Robert Nisbet, "Teggart of Berkeley," in *Masters: Portraits of Great Teachers*, ed. Joseph Epstein (New York: Basic Books, 1981), 73–74.

4. Mary Burgan with Michael Berger, "Teaching Literature: Rethinking the Socratic Method," in *Teaching Undergraduates: Essays from the Lilly Endowment Workshop on Liberal Arts*, ed. Bruce A. Kimball (Buffalo, N.Y.: Prometheus Books, 1988), 61.

5. Lionel Basney, "Teacher: Eleven Notes," *American Scholar* 71 (Winter 2002): 86.

6. I thank John Kasson, Department of History, University of North Carolina at Chapel Hill, for this insight.

7. University of North Carolina Center for Teaching and Learning, "Syllabus Development Guide," <http://devel.ctl.unc.edu/syllabus—guide/oinvitation.html> (July 2004).

8. Burgan, "Teaching Literature," 64.

9. In this respect, you mirror your future students, who will begin the course, whether they realize it or not, with a mental model of what history (or economics or literature) is. See chapter 2.

10. Donald J. Raleigh, Department of History, University of North Carolina at Chapel Hill.

Chapter Two

1. One-third of employed undergraduates hold full-time jobs. Usually, they are older than twenty-five and attend part-time at four-year colleges or community colleges. The remaining two-thirds work, on average, twenty-five hours per week. They are usually less than twenty-five years old and attend four-year colleges. Jacqueline E. King, "Too Many Students Are Holding Jobs for Too Many Hours," *Chronicle of Higher Education*, May 1, 1998, A72.

2. Bette LaSere Erickson and Diane Weltner Strommer, *Teaching College Freshmen* (San Francisco: Jossey-Bass, 1991), 59–61.

3. William G. Perry, "Different Worlds in the Same Classroom," in *Improving Learning: New Perspectives*, ed. Paul Ramsden (London: Kogan Page, 1988), 148.

4. This formulation is adapted from Robert J. Kloss, "A Nudge Is Best: Helping Students through the Perry Scheme of Intellectual Development," <http://honors.ucdavis.edu/fh/ct/kloss.html> (July 2004).

5. Mary Field Belenky, Blythe McVicker Clinchy, Nancy Rule Goldberger, and Jill Mattuck Tarule, *Women's Ways of Knowing: The Development of Self, Voice, and Mind* (1986; New York: Basic Books, 1997).

6. Mary Crawford, *Talking Difference: On Gender and Language* (London: Sage, 1995), esp. 96–99, 101–8, and chap. 4.

7. Ibid., 14.

8. Jack Niemonen, quoted in Dean S. Dorn, ed., *Voices from the Classroom: Interviews with Thirty-Six Sociologists about Teaching* (Washington, D.C.: American Sociological Association Teaching Resources Center, 1996), 232.

9. Spencer Downing, "Stories from Orlando," *Committee on Teaching Newsletter*, Spring 2002, Department of History, University of North Carolina at Chapel Hill.

10. bell hooks, *Teaching to Transgress: Education as the Practice of Freedom* (New York: Routledge, 1994), 186; Stephen D. Brookfield and Stephen Preskill, *Discussion as a Way of Teaching: Tools and Techniques for Democratic Classrooms* (San Francisco: Jossey-Bass, 1999), chap. 7.

11. Ira Shor, *When Students Have Power: Negotiating Authority in a Critical Pedagogy* (Chicago: University of Chicago Press, 1996), 6–7.

12. Castellano B. Turner, "Racial Problems in Society and in the Classroom," in *Achieving Against the Odds: How Academics Become Teachers of Diverse Students*, ed. Esther Kingston-Mann and Tim Sieber (Philadelphia: Temple University Press, 2001), 100–101.

13. Brookfield and Preskill, *Discussion*, 130.

14. My thanks to Lee Warren, Derek Bok Center for Teaching and Learning, Harvard University, for these ideas.

Chapter Three

1. Thanks to Ken Bain, New York University Center for Teaching Excellence, for this concept.

2. Frederick J. Oerther III, Department of Economics, Greensboro College, Greensboro, North Carolina.

3. Rashmi Varma, Department of English and Comparative Literary Studies, University of Warwick, United Kingdom.

4. Adapted from syllabi by Norman Hurley, Department of Political Science, and Terence McIntosh, Department of History, University of North Carolina at Chapel Hill.

5. Julia Wood, Department of Communication Studies, University of North Carolina at Chapel Hill.

6. Laura A. Janda, Department of Slavic Languages, University of North Carolina at Chapel Hill.

7. Adapted from James Leloudis, Department of History, University of North Carolina at Chapel Hill.

8. Barbara Harris, Department of History, University of North Carolina at Chapel Hill.

9. Gavin Campbell, Center for American Studies, Doshisha University, Kyoto, Japan.

Chapter Four

1. Paul Ramsden, "The Context of Learning," in *The Experience of Learning*, ed. Ference Marton, Dai Hounsell, and Noel Entwistle (Edinburgh: Scottish Academic Press, 1984), esp. 148–51; Joseph Lowman, *Mastering the Techniques of Teaching* (2d ed.; San Francisco: Jossey-Bass, 1995), 136–37.

2. Beverly Watkins, "More and More Professors in Many Academic Disciplines Routinely Require Students to Do Extensive Writing," *Chronicle of Higher Education*, July 18, 1990, A13–14, A16; S. K. Tollefson, *Encouraging Student Writing* (Berkeley: University of California Office of Educational Development, 1988).

3. See Bette LaSere Erickson and Diane Weltner Strommer, *Teaching College Freshmen* (San Francisco: Jossey-Bass, 1991), chap. 8; and David Royse, *Teaching Tips for College and University Instructors: A Practical Guide* (Boston: Allyn and Bacon, 2001), 47–50.

4. Laura L. Nash, "The Rhythms of the Semester," in *The Art and Craft*

of Teaching, ed. Margaret Morganroth Gullette (Cambridge, Mass.: Harvard University Press, 1984), chap. 6.

5. Daniel Bell, *The Reforming of General Education: The Columbia College Experience in Its National Setting* (Garden City, N.Y.: Anchor Books, 1968), 177–82.

6. Benjamin Bloom, *Cognitive Domain*, vol. 1 of *Taxonomy of Educational Objectives* (New York: McKay, 1956). For a helpful discussion of how to use the taxonomy, see Royse, *Teaching Tips*, 42–47.

7. Erickson and Strommer, *Teaching College Freshmen*, chap. 4. In certain fields one may need to rely on Bloom's taxonomy. In economics, for instance, *application* occurs when students use a particular economic tool (for example, marginal analysis) to work out a problem. But real economic thinking requires that students learn to choose the appropriate tools for the problem. Thinking at that level entails *analysis* and likely *synthesis*. I thank Michael Salemi, Department of Economics, University of North Carolina at Chapel Hill, for this insight.

8. I thank Erica Rothman for this clarification.

9. For a more detailed syllabus checklist, see the Syllabus Tutorial of the University of Minnesota Center for Teaching and Learning Services, <http://www1.umn.edu/ohr/teachlearn/syllabus/checklist.html> (July 2004).

Chapter Five

1. Joseph Katz, "Does Teaching Help Students Learn," in *Teaching Undergraduates: Essays from the Lilly Endowment Workshop on Liberal Arts*, ed. Bruce A. Kimball (Buffalo, N.Y.: Prometheus Books, 1988), 173. A national survey in 2000 of economics professors reported that the median amount of time spent lecturing was 83 percent; see William E. Becker and Michael Watts, "Teaching Economics at the Start of the 21st Century: Still Chalk-and-Talk," *American Economic Review* 91 (May 2001): 446–51.

2. Donald R. Bligh, *What's the Use of Lecturing?* (San Francisco: Jossey-Bass, 1998), chap. 1.

3. Vivien Hodgson, "Learning from Lectures," in *The Experience of Learning*, ed. Ference Marton, Dai Hounsell, and Noel Entwistle (Edinburgh: Scottish Academic Press, 1984), chap. 6, esp. 92–93.

4. Bligh, *What's the Use of Lecturing?*; J. Hartley and I. K. Davies, "Note-Taking: A Critical Review," *Programmed Learning and Educational Technology* 15 (1978): 207–24, cited in Wilbert J. McKeachie, "Improving Lectures by Understanding Students' Information Processing," *New Directions for Teaching and Learning* 2 (1980): 25–35.

5. Ken Bain, *What the Best College Teachers Do* (Cambridge, Mass.: Harvard University Press, 2004), 98–107.

6. David Kolb, *Experiential Learning: Experience as the Source of Learning and Development* (Englewood Cliffs, N.J.: Prentice-Hall, 1984); Bette LaSere Erickson and Diane Weltner Strommer, *Teaching College Freshmen* (San Francisco: Jossey-Bass, 1991), 68–69, 98–99.

7. Bain, *What the Best College Teachers Do*, 37.

8. I'm grateful to Leah Potter for clarifying my thinking.

9. I borrow the theater metaphor from Joseph Lowman, who elaborates it thoughtfully in *Mastering the Techniques of Teaching* (2d ed.; San Francisco: Jossey-Bass, 1995), chap. 4.

10. I'm grateful to Lee Warren for crystallizing these suggestions.

11. Lowman, *Mastering the Techniques of Teaching*, 136; J. R. Davis, *Teaching Strategies for the College Classroom* (Boulder, Colo.: Westview Press, 1976), cited by McKeachie, "Improving Lectures."

12. K. L. Ruhl, C. A. Hughes, and P. J. Schloss, "Using the Pause Procedure to Enhance Lecture Recall," *Teacher Education and Special Education* 10 (Winter 1987): 14–18. I thank Ed Neal for this citation.

Chapter Six

1. Adapted from Peter Filene, "Teaching the Children of the Vietnam War," *Journal of American History* 85 (March 1999): 1535–37.

2. Herman Sinaiko, "Energizing the Classroom: A Personal and Phenomenological View," in *Teaching Undergraduates: Essays from the Lilly Endowment Workshop on Liberal Arts*, ed. Bruce A. Kimball (Buffalo, N.Y.: Prometheus Books, 1988), 24–25.

3. For a detailed rationale of this approach, see W. Lee Hansen and Michael K. Salemi, "Improving Classroom Discussion in Economics Courses," in *Teaching Undergraduate Economics: A Handbook for Instructors*, ed. William B. Walstad and Phillip Saunders (New York: Irwin/ McGraw Hill, 1998), chap. 14.

4. See John Bransford et al., *How People Learn: Brain, Mind, Experience, and School* (Washington, D.C.: National Academy Press, 1999).

5. Stephen D. Brookfield and Stephen Preskill, *Discussion as a Way of Teaching: Tools and Techniques for Democratic Classrooms* (San Francisco: Jossey-Bass, 1999), 3, and chap. 1.

6. Jennifer Heath, Department of History, University of North Carolina at Chapel Hill.

7. Michael Hunt, Department of History, University of North Carolina at Chapel Hill.

8. Stanley Chojnacki, Department of History, University of North Carolina at Chapel Hill.

9. Theda Perdue, Department of History, University of North Carolina at Chapel Hill.

10. In history courses, for example, students invariably name white men who held political or military positions. You then ask them to discuss who is left out of their list and why they've been left out.

11. Donald M. Nonini, Department of Anthropology, University of North Carolina at Chapel Hill.

12. Judith Bennett, Department of History, University of North Carolina at Chapel Hill.

13. Alan Brinkley et al., *The Chicago Handbook for Teachers: A Practical Guide to the College Classroom* (Chicago: University of Chicago Press, 1999), 163–67.

14. Brookfield and Preskill, *Discussion as a Way of Teaching*, 49–50.

Chapter Seven

1. John C. Bean, *Engaging Ideas: The Professor's Guide to Integrating Writing, Critical Thinking, and Active Learning in the Classroom* (San Francisco: Jossey-Bass, 1996), 94–95, and chaps. 6 and 10.

2. Ibid., 178.

3. William Naumes and Margaret J. Naumes, *The Art and Craft of Case Writing* (Thousand Oaks, Calif.: Sage, 1999), 13.

4. John Boehrer and Marty Linsky, "Teaching with Cases: Learning to Question," in *The Changing Face of College Teaching*, ed. Marilla D. Svincki, in *New Directions for Teaching and Learning* 42 (Summer 1990): 41–57.

5. For a wide range of cases in the sciences, see the website of the National Center for Case Study Teaching in Science: <http://ublib.buffalo.edu/libraries/projects/cases/case.html> (July 2004). Another valuable source for political, historical, and military games is *Academic Gaming Review*: <http://www.gis.net/~pldr/> (July 2004). For case studies pertaining to ethics in diverse fields (business, science, psychology, and medicine), see Chowan College Center for Ethics: <http://www.chowan.edu/acadp/ethics/studies.htm>. For twenty sociological case studies, see the University of California, Santa Barbara, Department of Sociology website: <http://www.soc.ucsb.edu/projects/casemethod> (July 2004).

6. Adapted from Julia T. Wood, *Communication Mosaics: An Introduction to the Field of Communication* (3d ed.; Belmont, Calif.: Wadsworth, 2004), 95–96.

7. Wilbert J. McKeachie, *Teaching Tips: Strategies, Research, and Theory for College and University Teachers* (9th ed.; Lexington, Mass.: D. C. Heath, 1994), 160.

8. Thomas Bartlett, "What Makes a Teacher Great?" *Chronicle of Higher Education*, December 12, 2003, A8–9.

9. Ken Bain, *What the Best College Teachers Do* (Cambridge, Mass.: Harvard University Press, 2004), 60–63.

10. Lou Carpenter, formerly at Lincoln University, Jefferson City, Missouri.

11. Jonathan Young, formerly at University of North Carolina at Chapel Hill.

12. Adapted from the Lawrence Berkeley National Laboratory's Ethical, Legal, and Social Issues in Science (ELSI) Project. For the full text, including background information and links, see the ELSI Project website: <http://www.lbl.gov/Education/ELSI/ELSI.html> (July 2004).

13. State Appellate Defenders Office, *Criminal Defense Newsletter* 19 (September 1996), <http://www.sado.org/19cdn12.htm> (July 2004); National Institute of Justice, *Eyewitness Evidence: A Guide for Law Enforcement* (October 1999), <http://www.ojp.usdoj.gov/nij/pubs-sum/178240.htm> (July 2004).

14. Karen Chambers, Department of Psychology, Saint Mary's College, Notre Dame, Indiana, published by the National Center for Case Study Teaching in Science: <http://ublib.buffalo.edu/libraries/projects/cases/memory/memory.html> (July 2004).

Chapter Eight

1. The best source is John C. Bean, *Engaging Ideas: The Professor's Guide to Integrating Writing, Critical Thinking, and Active Learning in the Classroom* (San Francisco: Jossey-Bass, 1996). Also see Bette LaSere Erickson and Diane Weltner Strommer, *Teaching College Freshmen* (San Francisco: Jossey-Bass, 1991).

2. I thank David Holdzkom for helping me to clarify these issues.

3. Ken Bain, *What the Best College Teachers Do* (Cambridge, Mass.: Harvard University Press, 2004); Richard Light, *Making the Most of College: College Students Speak Their Minds* (Cambridge, Mass.: Harvard University Press, 2001).

4. Peter Kaufman, Department of Religious Studies, University of North Carolina at Chapel Hill.

5. Wilbert J. McKeachie, *Teaching Tips: Strategies, Research, and Theory for College and University Teachers* (9th ed.; Lexington, Mass.: D. C. Heath, 1994), 353–55; Joseph Lowman, *Mastering the Techniques of Teaching* (2d

ed.; San Francisco: Jossey-Bass, 1995), 230–31; Barbara Gross Davis, *Tools for Teaching* (San Francisco: Jossey-Bass, 2001), 198.

6. R. Ames and C. Ames, "Motivation and Effective Teaching," in *Dimensions of Thinking and Cognitive Instruction*, ed. B. F. Jones and L. Idol (Hillsdale, N.J.: Erlbaum, 1990), cited in Davis, *Tools for Teaching*, 197.

7. Edward Slavishak, Department of History, Susquehanna University.

8. Ken Bain, Center for Teaching Excellence and Department of History, New York University.

9. Robert E. Weir, "Empowering Students While Cutting Corners: Efficient Grading of History Essays," *Perspectives* 31 (March 1993): 6.

10. Lex Newman, Course Portfolio, Philosophy 101, University of Nebraska at Lincoln, <http://www.unl.edu/peerrev/newmanPfolio.html> (July 2004).

11. If you want a more detailed discussion of questions and answers in student evaluations, read Davis, *Tools for Teaching*, chap. 48.

12. David Royse, *Teaching Tips for College and University Instructors: A Practical Guide* (Boston: Allyn and Bacon, 2001), 260.

13. Mark Edmundson, "On the Uses of a Liberal Education: I. As Lite Entertainment for Bored College Students," *Harper's Magazine* 295 (September 1997): 39–40.

14. Lowman, *Mastering the Techniques of Teaching*, 257; Royse, *Teaching Tips*, 262.

15. Davis, *Tools for Teaching*, 397. See also McKeachie, *Teaching Tips*, 317, 326.

16. Adapted from Erika Lindemann, *A Rhetoric for Writing Teachers* (4th ed.; New York: Oxford University Press, 2001), 239–42.

17. Richard Derderian, formerly in Department of History, University of North Carolina at Chapel Hill.

18. Richard Froyen and Michael Salemi, Department of Economics, University of North Carolina at Chapel Hill.

Chapter Nine

1. Willie Morris, *North Toward Home* (New York: Houghton Mifflin, 1967), 163–64.

2. Ken Bain, *What the Best College Teachers Do* (Cambridge, Mass.: Harvard University Press, 2004), chap. 6.

3. I thank Lee Warren, Derek Bok Center for Teaching and Learning, Harvard University, for this idea.

4. I'm grateful to Robert Johnston, Department of History, University of Illinois, Chicago, for his suggestions.

Chapter Ten

1. David Riesman, Daniel Bell, Helen Vendler, and Stephen Jay Gould, "Balancing Teaching and Writing," *On Teaching and Learning: The Journal of the Harvard-Danforth Center* 2 (January 1987): 15–16.

2. John A. Goldsmith, John Komlos, and Penny Schine Gold, *The Chicago Guide to Your Academic Career: A Portable Mentor for Scholars from Graduate School through Tenure* (Chicago: University of Chicago Press, 2001), 164.

3. Glenn Goodwin, quoted in Dean S. Dorn, ed., *Voices from the Classroom: Interviews with Thirty-Six Sociologists about Teaching* (Washington, D.C.: American Sociological Association Teaching Resources Center, 1996), 72.

4. Laura Nathan, Mills College, quoted in ibid., 205. See also Jack Niemonen, University of South Dakota, quoted in ibid., 230. According to David Newman, a professor at DePauw since 1989: "It [DePauw] prides itself on the quality of its teaching. It's a place where people talk about teaching experiences in the hallway. I never heard this before at [the University of] Washington or [University of] Connecticut [at Storrs]. It really was an astounding thing to hear when I first heard it. People sharing ideas with each other. Professors sitting in on each other's classes. It was amazing." Ibid., 213.

5. Sheila Cordray, quoted in ibid., 42–43. See also Kichiro Iwamoto, Santa Clara University: "I got tenure back in the old days and frankly I said, 'I wasn't going to do this [publish].' They wanted an article per year. . . . I can see now with our new faculty the pressure is on them to do research and to publish." Ibid., 127.

6. Bruce A. Kimball, "Historia Calamitatum," in *Teaching Undergraduates: Essays from the Lilly Endowment Workshop on Liberal Arts*, ed. Bruce A. Kimball (Buffalo, N.Y.: Prometheus Books, 1988), 18.

7. Quoted in Dorn, *Voices from the Classroom*, 218.

8. For example, Sascha Feinstein, "From a Suicide, Some Lessons about the Spirit of Teaching and Academe's Political Burdens," *Chronicle of Higher Education*, January 16, 1991, B2; Scott Heller, "Teaching Awards: Aid to Tenure or Kiss of Death?" *Chronicle of Higher Education*, March 16, 1988, A14; Kimball, "Historia Calamitatum," 15.

9. Laura Nathan, quoted in Dorn, *Voices from the Classroom*, 205–6.

10. Goldsmith, Komlos, and Gold, *Chicago Guide to Your Academic Career*, 275.

11. Nancy Greenwood, quoted in Dorn, *Voices from the Classroom*, 97. For similar comments about service, see ibid., 205–6, 243. Also see Piper

Fogg, "So Many Committees, So Little Time," *Chronicle of Higher Education*, December 19, 2003, A14–15.

12. Andy Arnold, "Recent Graduates: Adventures in Teaching," *Committee on Teaching Newsletter*, Winter 2003, Department of History, University of North Carolina at Chapel Hill.

13. For a thorough and instructive discussion of these matters, see Goldsmith, Komlos, and Gold, *Chicago Guide to Your Academic Career*, chap. 6.

14. Arnold, "Recent Graduates."

15. The breakdown is as follows: teaching in class—8 hours; class preparation—19; office hours—1; research/scholarship—12; administration/service—11; outside consulting—1. Goldsmith, Komlos, and Gold, *Chicago Guide to Your Academic Career*, 275.

16. Ibid., 138.

17. I thank Daniel Anderson, Department of English, University of North Carolina at Chapel Hill, for this metaphorical insight.

18. Quoted in Dorn, *Voices from the Classroom*, 96. Of course, many faculty disagree.

19. I observed this presentation by Lisa Lindsay, Department of History, University of North Carolina at Chapel Hill.

20. My thanks to Bill Van Norman and Michael Hunt, Department of History, University of North Carolina at Chapel Hill, for these perspectives.

21. Quoted in Dorn, *Voices from the Classroom*, 243.

If You Want to Learn More
A Selected, Annotated Bibliography

GENERAL GUIDES

Bain, Ken. *What the Best College Teachers Do.* Cambridge, Mass.: Harvard University Press, 2004.

What do the best teachers do that makes such a difference in the lives and intellectual development of their students? The product of fifteen years of study, this little volume will help you explore the thinking and practices of professors, in a variety of disciplines, who have had enormous success in helping and encouraging their students to achieve remarkable learning results. It will help you examine general principles that you can adopt and will provide you with individual stories of outstanding teachers. You will discover that the best teachers have powerful ways of understanding what it means to learn in their disciplines, how best to foster learning, and how they and their students can best understand the nature and progress of the learning. Be prepared to turn your thinking upside down.

Davis, Barbara Gross. *Tools for Teaching.* San Francisco: Jossey-Bass, 2001.

This encyclopedic reference book deserves to be on your bookshelf for those moments—and there will be many—when you need a quick answer to a quandary. Do you want to personalize a large lecture class, devise problem sets for homework, use a flipchart, or write a letter of recommendation? In forty-nine topical chapters, each divided into countless, easy-to-identify subtopics, Davis dispenses brisk, clear, and evenhanded analysis. Trained as an educational psychologist, she also cites a lot of empirical data, backed up by copious bibliographies. Part of the book is available online at
<http://teaching.berkeley.edu/bgd/teaching.html> (July 2004).

Erickson, Bette LaSere, and Diane Weltner Strommer. *Teaching College Freshmen.* San Francisco: Jossey-Bass, 1991.

If you are teaching first-year students, you should consult this thoughtful, readable book. The authors, both professors at the University of Rhode Island, have a knack for translating cognitive theories and psychological typologies into laypersons' language. Better yet, they show you how to put these concepts to work in sample writing assignments and exam questions from diverse fields (art, physics, history, et al.). If you enjoy thinking about thinking, you'll appreciate this book.

Goldsmith, John A., John Komlos, and Penny Schine Gold. *The Chicago Guide to Your Academic Career: A Portable Mentor for Scholars from Graduate School through Tenure.* Chicago: University of Chicago Press, 2001.

This book offers "a user's guide to academic life." As you read the transcribed informal discussion among three scholars, you will find insiders' frank perspectives on how to complete your dissertation, land an academic job, navigate the pedagogical and political challenges of your department, and obtain tenure.

Lowman, Joseph. *Mastering the Techniques of Teaching.* 2d ed. San Francisco: Jossey-Bass, 1995.

In this gracefully written book Lowman provides thoughtful advice on the full range of issues that confront college teachers. As a psychologist, he is especially sensitive to the interpersonal dynamics of a classroom, analyzing how different techniques affect students' motivation for better and worse. If you want to improve what you do in the classroom, see the interesting chapter on teaching as a dramatic performance.

McKeachie, Wilbert J. *Teaching Tips: Strategies, Research, and Theory for College and University Teachers.* 11th ed. Lexington, Mass.: D. C. Heath, 2002.

Now in its eleventh edition and still going strong, McKeachie's book has earned nearly biblical status. He and his coauthors offer balanced, earnest advice on every aspect of teaching, from leading your first discussion, to using audiovisual equipment, to controlling cheating. They smoothly blend day-to-day practice with cognitive theory. More of a manual than a reference book, it complements Davis's *Tools for Teaching* as a bookend on your pedagogical shelf.

THEORY

Andre, Rae, and Peter J. Frost, eds. *Researchers Hooked on Teaching: Noted Scholars Discuss the Synergies of Teaching and Research.* Thousand Oaks, Calif.: Sage, 1996.

How can you balance the often seemingly conflicting demands of teaching and research? The contributors to this collection of essays, all leading scholars, tell you how they do it. They collectively argue that you must both balance and integrate the two enterprises if you want to have a notable academic career that includes success in both areas.

Barr, Robert B., and John Tagg. "From Teaching to Learning: A New Paradigm for Undergraduate Education." *Change* 27 (November/December 1995): 12–25.

In this widely reprinted article, the authors take a lot of emerging ideas about teaching and learning and suggest, as the title implies, that together they represent a whole new way of thinking about undergraduate education. The "new paradigm" suggested here will help you understand and appreciate the rich fabric of ideas and practices discussed in other works.

Bransford, John, et al. *How People Learn: Brain, Mind, Experience, and School.* Washington, D.C.: National Academy Press, 1999.

If you want to understand what the learning sciences have discovered about human learning and the implications those findings have for the way we teach, this is the place to start. A group of leading scientists summarize what we know about how people learn and how some exemplary teachers have used those insights to foster deep learning in students. Many of the examples are drawn from working with children, but the insights into human learning have powerful implications for what we teach our college students, how we teach them, and how we understand and assess their learning.

Cross, Patricia, and Mimi Harris Steadman. *Classroom Research: Implementing the Scholarship of Teaching.* San Francisco: Jossey-Bass, 1996.

You are a good researcher, so why not use good research techniques to assess the quality of your teaching? This book will enable you to do just that, helping you raise powerful questions about teaching and learning in your classroom, explore some of the existing research on the issues, and design a systematic way to collect information from your students.

Light, Greg, and Roy Cox. *Learning and Teaching in Higher Education: The Reflective Professional.* London: Paul Chapman, 2001.

If you had a decade to explore the vast body of research and theoretical literature on learning and teaching and wanted to summarize its most important findings, this is the book you would probably produce. It is both a serious challenger to McKeachie's biblical status (in that it covers everything) and an important theoretical work. Written by two scholars at the University of London, one of whom (Light) now directs the Searle Center for Teaching Excellence at Northwestern University, the book will help you focus on learning—yours and your students'—and will give you a vocabulary for thinking about the challenges we face in promoting learning in the increasingly complex world of higher education.

PRACTICES

Bean, John C. *Engaging Ideas: The Professor's Guide to Integrating Writing, Critical Thinking, and Active Learning in the Classroom*. San Francisco: Jossey-Bass, 1996.

As you browse through this volume, you will be astonished by the many kinds of stimulating assignments that had never occurred to you. "Critical" and "active" are the key concepts. Bean provides a compendium of opportunities, especially formal and informal writings, cases, and small-group exercises. He also offers exceptionally lucid discussion about the connection between thinking and writing, as well as about the process of "coaching" students to improve as thinkers/writers.

Brookfield, Stephen D., and Stephen Preskill. *Discussion as a Way of Teaching: Tools and Techniques for Democratic Classrooms*. San Francisco: Jossey-Bass, 1999.

The title is misleading. Brookfield and Preskill believe that discussion is *the* way to teach. With exceptional cogency and passion, they explore the intellectual, personal, and ethical dimensions of discussion. Scenarios from their own classes bring these abstractions to life. As a particularly interesting emphasis, they suggest inventive techniques for eliciting student feedback.

Bruffee, Kenneth A. *Collaborative Learning: Higher Education, Interdependence, and the Authority of Knowledge*. Baltimore: Johns Hopkins University Press, 1993.

Bruffee will help you develop highly effective ways to employ collaborative learning, but he will also challenge you to rethink how we understand education. He argues that we construct what we think we understand in communities of "knowledgeable peers." Students must negotiate the boundaries around the communities they are trying to join (such as academic disciplines), and they can best do that with systematic practice in working collaboratively on real intellectual issues to construct knowledge the way their professors do.

Christensen, C. Roland, David A. Garvin, and Ann Sweet, eds. *Education for Judgment: The Artistry of Discussion Leadership*. Boston: Harvard Business School Press, 1991.

These personal essays focus on using discussion to help students learn how to make judgments. They will help you explore both the practical, nitty-gritty questions and the broad philosophical issues of this approach. Each contributor takes you on a journey through the pleasures and frustrations of teaching by way of discussion, identifying ideas and practices that produce the most powerful learning environments. You can explore a range of topics, including ways to use discussion to help students learn technical material and how to set ground rules for good discussions. The editors believe that it is possible to identify the elements of exceptional teaching and to help other people employ those elements.

Finkel, Donald L. *Teaching with Your Mouth Shut*. Portsmouth, N.H.: Boynton/Cook, 2000.

Why should you avoid teaching by talking? And even if you want to avoid "telling," how would you do it and still have your students learn? Finkel offers fervent answers, drawing upon his interdisciplinary teaching at Evergreen College. By reporting and interpreting scenes and conversations from his classes, he shows (and tells) you how he kept his mouth shut and let books, writing assignments, problems, and students perform the teaching.

Schank, Roger C., and Chip Cleary. *Engines for Education*. Mahwah, N.J.: Lawrence Erlbaum, 1995.

Can you create a learning environment in which each student pursues her or his own interest, an intriguing environment that captures attention and provides individual help "just in time," only as people develop a "need to know"? Schank, a learning scientist, and one of his former graduate students show you how to do that in this iconoclastic exploration of what's wrong with schools on all levels and how technology can fix it. This work practices what it preaches. You can read it as a standard book, or you can explore its ideas online in a hypertext book, an option that gives you complete control over what you learn and in what order. If you are interested in using the World Wide Web and computers, this is the place to start thinking about what you might do. You can find the Web version at <http://engines4ed.org/hyperbook/nodes/intro-zoomer.html> (July 2004).

Walvoord, Barbara E., and Virginia Johnson Anderson. *Effective Grading: A Tool for Learning and Assessment*. San Francisco: Jossey-Bass, 1998.

How you grade can either reinforce all your good efforts or sabotage your teaching, sending messages you never intend about what kind of learning you expect in the class. Walvoord, an English professor at

Notre Dame, and Anderson, a biology professor at Towson State, help you craft good assignments, motivate students, link grades to intellectual standards, and provide useful feedback to students. They also provide some useful ideas about using the grading process to assess the institution and the curriculum, ideas that may come in handy in a few years when your dean appoints you to a committee to address such matters.

VARIOUS DISCIPLINES

Economics

Salemi, Michael K. "An Illustrated Case for Active Learning." *Southern Economic Journal* 68 (January 2002): 721–31.
  Using the concept of "present value," the author demonstrates how to involve financial markets students in order to undertake active rather than passive learning.
Saunders, Phillip, and William B. Walstad, eds. *Teaching Undergraduate Economics: A Handbook for Instructors.* New York: Irwin/McGraw Hill, 1998.
  This updated collection of twenty-two articles, written by distinguished professors nationwide, discusses a variety of topics under four rubrics: goals and objectives, learning theory, instructional methods, and evaluation. Whether a new or experienced instructor of economics, you will benefit from the blend of theory, empirical research, and practical application.

English

College Composition and Communication (periodical).
College English (periodical). <http://www.ncte.org/pubs/journals/ce> (July 2004).
Connors, Robert, and Cheryl Glenn. *The New St. Martin's Guide to Teaching Writing.* Boston: Bedford/St. Martin's, 1999.
  For a someone who is going to teach a first-year composition course for the first time, this book will be instructive and reassuring. The initial chapters walk you through the opening weeks of class, followed by chapters explaining in lucid detail how to design assignments and evaluations. The advice is compassionate but not condescending, sensible but sophisticated. The last third of the book reprints a baker's dozen of lively, influential articles that link practice and theory. The

middle third, by contrast, is suitable only for experienced teachers. Here the authors discuss complex theories pertaining to rhetoric and composition.

Lindemann, Erika. *A Rhetoric for Writing Teachers*. 4th ed. New York: Oxford University Press, 2001.

There is more information and insight packed into this book than you will need or can digest in the short run. Consult the chapters that matter most to you. Lindemann is particularly creative and useful when discussing diverse kinds of writing assignments as well as evaluation techniques. Daniel Anderson contributes a valuable chapter on how to use the World Wide Web as a pedagogical tool.

University of Chicago Writing Program. "The Little Red Schoolhouse Writing Guide." <http://writing-program.uchicago.edu/schoolhouse/index.htm> (July 2004).

Different sections of this highly original and provocative guide to writing appear online every time the course is taught at the University of Chicago, but they don't stay up for long. There are some extraordinarily effective exercises in this guide that will help your students write more successfully.

Geology

Journal of Geological and Related Sciences (periodical).

History

American Social History Project, "History Matters." <http://historymatters.gmu.edu/> (July 2004).

This is the place to go if you want a shortcut to primary sources: written (typically four or five pages of text), visual (cartoons, photos, and videos), and audio (speeches). These sources deal with a wide range of dramatic events and issues in American history. With almost one thousand choices from the seventeenth century to the present, you surely will find something suitable for your course. Capsule descriptions expedite the search.

But that's not all in this pedagogical treasure chest. This site also includes guides to instruct students how to analyze these primary sources; articles by historians discussing and interpreting events; an annotated list of hundreds of historical websites; and annotated syllabi of history courses.

"Best of History Websites." <http://besthistorysites.net/> (July 2004).

As the title indicates, you will find links to websites for virtually every historical era, region, and nation. Better yet, the sites are annotated, so you will be less likely to waste your time in mediocre or irrelevant browsing. There are also links to lesson plans, although these tend to be aimed at secondary school teachers.

The History Teacher (periodical).

Stearns, Peter N., Peter Seixas, and Sam Wineburg, eds. *Knowing, Teaching, and Learning History: National and International Perspectives.* New York: New York University Press, 2000.

In this collection of essays, historians address disparate topics from various perspectives, some leaning toward pedagogy and others toward content. If you're wanting ideas to incorporate into your course design, you should turn to the final six chapters. Stearns's analysis of his world history course is notably cogent and specific.

Teaching History: A Journal of Methods (periodical).

Wineburg, Sam. *Historical Thinking and Other Unnatural Acts: Charting the Future of Teaching the Past.* Philadelphia: Temple University Press, 2001.

Wineburg, a professor of history as well as cognitive psychology, attacks from many angles the question of how people understand the past differently. The most interesting answers emerge from several social-psychological experiments he constructed. With engaging vivacity, he reports, for example, how a group of teachers and a group of students found different "truths" in the same textbook chapter. Another essay discusses how youngsters (literally) pictured Pilgrims, western settlers, and hippies. These localized cases provoke Wineburg (and will provoke you) to ponder the subjectivity of historical understanding.

Philosophy and Religion

Teaching Philosophy (periodical).
<http://www.pdcnet.org/teachph.html> (July 2004).
Wabash Center. "Guide to Internet Resources for Teaching and Learning in Theology and Religion."
<http://www.wabashcenter.wabash.edu/internet/front.htm> (July 2004).

Physics

Arons, Arnold B. *A Guide to Introductory Physics Teaching.* New York: John Wiley, 1990.

Don't miss the chapter on critical thinking, even if you don't teach physics. It will provoke humanists, social and natural scientists to ponder what it means to think critically in their disciplines and how they might help students learn to do so. Arons, a physicist at the University of Washington, who became interested in how people learn physics, founded and headed the physics education project and helped revolutionize thinking about science education.

Psychology

Brody, Roz, and Nicky Hayes. *Teaching Introductory Psychology*. East Sussex, U.K.: Lawrence Erlbaum, 1995.

In this concise volume the authors briskly outline ideas for how to teach six areas of introductory psychology. Following a chapter on basic principles, they describe activities to engage students, as well as "practical work" involving straightforward research designs and statistical analysis. You will find particularly useful the sets of essay questions for each of the six areas. Finally, the "modules" for six-week, eight-week, and full-length introductory courses offer a handy starting point for deciding what you want or need to "cover."

Sternberg, Robert J., ed. *Teaching Introductory Psychology: Survival Tips from the Experts*. Washington, D.C.: American Psychological Association, 1997.

This collection of essays nicely complements Brody and Hayes's book. Eleven experienced teachers of psychology deliver thoughtful, candid ideas about a wide range of topics, including pedagogical principles, critical thinking, large classes, integration of research and teaching, and the role of passion.

Teaching of Psychology (periodical).

Sociology

Dorn, Dean S., ed. *Voices from the Classroom: Interviews with Thirty-Six Sociologists about Teaching*. Washington, D.C.: American Sociological Association Teaching Resources Center, 1996.

You don't need to be a sociologist to find these interviews fascinating. These faculty members may not "tell all" about their situations and feelings as teachers, but they tell a remarkable amount with instructive, sometimes startling candor. Veterans and newcomers, teaching in diverse large and small institutions around the country, they give you an inside look at our profession. They give special attention, of course, to the issues and methodologies of teaching sociology.

McKinney, Kathleen. *Sociology through Active Learning.* Thousand Oaks, Calif.: Sage, 2001.

If you want to build active learning into your course, this student handbook is your best bet. It provides instructions and worksheets for fifty exercises in ten topic areas such as theory and methods, socialization and interaction, stratification, organizations and bureaucracy, race and gender and sexual orientation, deviance and crime, and collective behavior.

You may adapt the exercises to your courses, but they are so well designed that you can easily use them "as is." Indeed, you can construct an entire course around this book.

The invaluable accompanying instructor's manual describes each exercise, with information about the context and purpose, as well as suggested methods and time use. (I thank Howard Aldrich for this citation and review.)

Teaching Sociology (periodical).

<http://www.asanet.org/pubs/journsub.html#TS> (July 2004).

LINKS TO PEDAGOGICAL SITES AND SYLLABI

Center for History and New Media,

<http://chnm.gmu.edu/tools/syllabi/> (July 2004).

This website offers you literally thousands of syllabi of college courses across the country. You can search by keyword for the particular subjects you want.

University of North Carolina at Chapel Hill, Department of Sociology, <http://www.unc.edu/~healdric/Home9.html>.

This website, created by Professor Howard Aldrich, includes several valuable links to educational sites, including how to detect plagiarism, to use e-mail discussion groups, and to build Web-based tools; cooperative learning websites, including reading lists and how-to-do-it pages; the case method site of the University of California at Santa Barbara Sociology Department, which includes twenty cases, as well as instructions on how to create your own cases; and e-books, online books, and other technologies. Look here for websites such as Open Mind, ebrary, Questia, and other sites that will give you access to content, often for free.

TEACHING AND LEARNING CENTERS

There are more than a hundred centers for teaching. I list a few whose websites offer particularly instructive and varied resources (all were accessed in July 2004). Many of the others also will be useful, so please don't limit yourself to the ones below.

Brown University Sheridan Center for Teaching and Learning, <http://www.brown.edu/Administration/Sheridan—Center>.

Among its many services, this site provides help in developing a syllabus and creating a teaching portfolio.

Harvard University Bok Center for Teaching and Learning, <http://bokcenter.harvard.edu>.

Here you will find invaluable videotape clips of good teaching.

New York University Center for Teaching Excellence, <http://www.nyu.edu/cte/www.html>.

This website provides links to books, articles, and sites spanning a wide range of topics, including how humans learn and how students approach learning, teaching and learning in specific disciplines, issues in science education, technology, and problem-based learning.

Northwestern University Searle Center for Teaching Excellence, <http://president.scfte.northwestern.edu>.

Read their newsletters.

Princeton University McGraw Center for Teaching Excellence, <http://web.princeton.edu/sites/mcgraw/index.html>.

Look at their "McGraw Minigraphs": one-page introductions to important topics in teaching and learning that distill recent research and provide "some 'how-to' tips."

University at Buffalo Center for Teaching and Learning Resources, <http://wings.buffalo.edu/ctlr>.

This site gives you links to useful information on various subjects: interactive teaching in the field of engineering; problem-based learning; contending with plagiarism; teaching portfolios; and others.

University of Hawaii, Honolulu Community College, <http://honolulu.hawaii.edu/intranet/committees/FacDevCom/guidebk/teachtip/teachtip.htm>.

This website offers a huge and excellent string of articles online.

University of Iowa Center for Teaching, <www.uiowa.edu/~centeach/resources/index.html>.

You will find well-chosen, annotated links to teaching journals for a wide range of disciplines.

University of Massachusetts, Amherst, Center for Teaching, <http://www.umass.edu/cft/>.

This site provides useful suggestions about readings.

University of Michigan Center for Research on Learning and Teaching, <http://www.crlt.umich.edu>.

This site provides invaluable links not only to material on pedagogical topics, but especially to teaching resources for whatever discipline you are working in.

University of Minnesota Center for Teaching and Learning Services, <http://www1.umn.edu/ohr/teachlearn/>.

This center offers exceptionally helpful categories (critical thinking, mentoring, etc). In addition, you'll find excellent how-to lists, copies of *Teaching Professor*, and links to other pedagogy sites.

University of North Carolina at Chapel Hill Center for Teaching and Learning, <http://ctl.unc.edu>.

The center's two dozen pamphlets, the "For Your Consideration" series, offer crisp, thoughtful guidance on topics ranging from how to put together an effective course packet to what to do on your first day of class.

Vanderbilt University Center for Teaching, <http://www.vanderbilt.edu/cft>.

Here you'll find informative newsletters on various topics: diversity, reinvigorating a classroom, and teaching strategies, among others.

Index

Grading, 39, 119–20; of attendance, 62–63, 64; as control,
63; of discussion questions,
69–70; as evaluation, 93–94;
of teaching, 93–94; of teaching
and learning, 95–97; grading
curve, 97–98; as incentive,
98–99, 107; grading policies,
98–100; criteria (rubrics) for,
100–102, 111–12; shortcuts for,
102–4. *See also* Evaluation

Hall, Jacquelyn, 81
Harris, Barbara, 28–29
History, teaching of, 28–29, 30–
31, 42, 57–58, 76; games in,
83–86; sources for, 151–52, 154
Humanities, 42

Interviewing, 80

Learning: active learning, 2, 54–
55, 61, 76–82; as environment,
3; styles of, 15–16, 49–50; surface learning, 35; theories of,
146–48. *See also* Cognitive
skills; Cognitive stages
Lecturing: advantages of, 47–48;
disadvantages of, 48; keys to
success of, 49–51; as performance, 51–52; organization of,
52–53, 127; diversification of,
53–55; shortcuts to, 127; and
classroom technology, 127–29
Light, Richard, 97

Mathematics, 42
McKeachie, Wilbert J., 80
Mental models, 14, 22, 31, 61, 64,
133
Morris, Willie, 115

Newman, Lex, 104

Objectives. *See* Syllabi
Office hours, 117–21, 129–30, 131

Perfectionism, 29, 126–29, 133
Performance, teaching as, 52
Perry, William G., 16–17
Personal life, 125, 133
Philosophy, 59, 152
Physics, 152–53
Political science, 26, 77, 78
PowerPoint. *See* Technology,
classroom
Psychology: "meeting of the
minds" panel, 77; case study,
88–91; bibliography, 153
Publishing. *See* Scholarship and
teaching

Race, 19–20, 124; and lesson
plan, 67–69; student exhibit
on, 81
Reconstruction game, 84–86
Relationships, teacher-student:
and lectures, 47; outside of
class, 116–21, 129–30
Richardson, Chad, 81
Role-playing and simulation
games, 76–78, 83–88
Rubrics, 100–102, 111–12. *See
also* Evaluation; Feedback,
student

Scholarship and teaching, 122–
25, 133
Sciences, 42, 81, 86–88
Scientific research game, 86–88
Scott, Anne, 60
Self-reflection: by teachers, 1, 7,
11, 56; by students, 54–55

Sexual harassment, 120. *See also* Relationships, teacher-student
Sociology, 81, 153–54
Standards, maintaining, 3, 68, 69, 102
Students: characteristics of, 13–20, 136 (n. 1); relationships with teachers, 116–21, 129–30
Syllabi: "promising" syllabi, 23; defining aims in, 23–31, 36, 43; voice in, 26–28; defining outcomes in, 26–31, 36; calendar in, 36, 40; organization of, 37–38, 40; assignments in, 39, 41; nuts and bolts of, 39, 45, 46; setting rhythm in, 41–42; and web page, 128; website resources for, 154

Teaching: as dialogue, 2, 13, 50, 51, 61, 93–94, 132–33; styles of, 8–10; Socratic teaching, 9–10, 11, 69; philosophy of, 10–12, 24–25; communication skills

for, 47–54; as control, 98–100, 102; beyond classroom, 115–16, 118–21; versus publishing, 122–24, 130; as gratification, 126
Teaching and learning centers, 29, 108, 155–56
Teaching awards, 124
Technology, classroom, 54, 127–29; and discussion, 70–71; and videotaping, 108
Textbooks, 51

Values, social and ethical, 10, 28
Vietnam War, discussion of, 57–58

Web, World Wide, 54, 128, 151–52. *See also* Technology, classroom
Weir, Robert, 103–4
Women, 17–18, 124. *See also* Gender
Work schedule, 125, 130

H. Eugene and Lillian Youngs Lehman Series

Lamar Cecil, *Wilhelm II: Prince and Emperor, 1859–1900* (1989).

Carolyn Merchant, *Ecological Revolutions: Nature, Gender, and Science in New England* (1989).

Gladys Engel Lang and Kurt Lang, *Etched in Memory: The Building and Survival of Artistic Reputation* (1990).

Howard Jones, *Union in Peril: The Crisis over British Intervention in the Civil War* (1992).

Robert L. Dorman, *Revolt of the Provinces: The Regionalist Movement in America* (1993).

Peter N. Stearns, *Meaning Over Memory: Recasting the Teaching of Culture and History* (1993).

Thomas Wolfe, *The Good Child's River*, edited with an introduction by Suzanne Stutman (1994).

Warren A. Nord, *Religion and American Education: Rethinking a National Dilemma* (1995).

David E. Whisnant, *Rascally Signs in Sacred Places: The Politics of Culture in Nicaragua* (1995).

Lamar Cecil, *Wilhelm II: Emperor and Exile, 1900–1941* (1996).

Jonathan Hartlyn, *The Struggle for Democratic Politics in the Dominican Republic* (1998).

Louis A. Pérez Jr., *On Becoming Cuban: Identity, Nationality, and Culture* (1999).

Yaakov Ariel, *Evangelizing the Chosen People: Missions to the Jews in America, 1880–2000* (2000).

Philip F. Gura, *C. F. Martin and His Guitars, 1796–1873* (2003).

Louis A. Pérez Jr., *To Die in Cuba: Suicide and Society* (2005).

Peter Filene, *The Joy of Teaching: A Practical Guide for New College Instructors* (2005).